THE UNDERPRIVILEGED NATIONS

THE
UNDERPRIVILEGED
NATIONS

originally published in French under the title of
LES NATIONS PROLETAIRES

by

Pierre Moussa

Graduate of the Ecole Normale Superieure
Professor of Literature
Inspector of Finances

Translated from the French by Alan Braley

BEACON PRESS   BOSTON

TO MY WIFE

PUBLISHER'S NOTE

Throughout the text there are frequent references to BLACK AFRICA. By this term the author means all those territories south of the Sahara where French is spoken. With the exception of the former Belgian colonies these are territories in which the author has served as an administrator.

CONTENTS

Page

Introduction   ix

PART I
THE EXPLOITATION OF THE POORER NATIONS

CHAPTER I
Impoverishment of the have-not Nations?   3

CHAPTER II
Joseph's Policy   11

CHAPTER III
"Fifty-fifty"   23

CHAPTER IV
Agrarian Reform   40

CHAPTER V
From Middleman to Co-operative   51

CHAPTER VI
Malthus and the Underprivileged Nations   58

PART II
WAYS OF GROWTH

CHAPTER VII
Conditions of Growth   71

CHAPTER VIII
Savings in poor Countries   78

CHAPTER IX   *Page*
"The Lord will provide"   91

CHAPTER X
The Role of Private Capital   106

CHAPTER XI
Elements of a Technology of Development   131

CHAPTER XII
Intellectual Aid   141

CHAPTER XIII
Psychological and political Conditions   154

PART III

THE POLITICS AND GEOPOLITICS OF DEVELOPMENT

CHAPTER XIV
The Political Stakes   165

CHAPTER XV
The Economic Stakes   173

CHAPTER XVI
World Aid for a World Problem   180

Bibliography   193

INTRODUCTION

An old fable from the Cameroons tells how God went walking together with His three sons, a white man, a black man, and a gorilla. The last two lost their way and God went on walking with the white man only. This myth illustrates the black man's dream, the dream of getting away from a condition which he regards as almost animal, back to the white man, to God, to prosperity, to happiness.

If we enlarge this dream to take in not only the black world, but also all the inhabitants of the so-called underdeveloped or insufficiently developed countries, can it come true? If so, on what conditions, and how can the developed countries best help to make it come true? That is what this book is about.

What is an underdeveloped country? The word implies a relativity; it indicates that the country has attained a lower stage of development—but lower than what? Than what is possible, or than what is necessary, or lower than other countries? Let us pursue these three lines of thought.

Is it correct to describe as underdeveloped, a country which has not reached that stage of development made possible by its natural resources, which leaves potential sources of wealth untapped? This definition does indeed apply to the countries we call underdeveloped, but it is not true of such countries alone. Canada undoubtedly has more unexploited riches than most other countries in the world. France herself "has to be re-discovered and even re-colonized."[1]

It would be fair to say that the idea of underdevelopment has come full circle. The West has observed underdevelopment on the other continents, and then, looking at itself, has become aware of hidden aspects of underdevelopment within. In France, particularly, this gives rise to much thought around the concept of a "critical zone" or "French desert", which led to the formation of regional development companies and to much effort to advance the backward regions. In fact, through seeing the beam in the eye of the African, the Asiatic and the Latin American, we become aware of the mote of underdevelopment in our own eye.

It is significant that the last of the five Bureaux of Mines to be set up on French territory as an autonomous organization was in Metropolitan France (known as the Bureau for Geological, Geophysical and Mineral Research). Historically, France's search for raw materials began outside her frontiers, in North Africa, and particularly in Morocco. This is not only because the landscape is so denuded that it shows its bones, so to say; nor is it solely due to decisive action taken by certain men, such as Monsieur Eirik Labonne and his team, who were enthusiasts for the idea of mineral development at a time when it was not yet fashionable, and of whom Anatole de Monzie said: "He was a subterranean imperialist—a mining one". It was also because Frenchmen appeared to be thinking subconsciously: "Obviously in a country of mature civilization like our own, whatever is there to be found must have been found already; let us look for new things in new continents". So whereas Labonne built up a mining empire, it was their empire that made the French miners. Many Frenchmen would have been astonished to have been told in 1938 that France had seams of coal which had not been discovered, or that oil would gush in Aquitaine.

The West discovered the idea of underdevelopment far from its own shores and has experimented there with methods of de-

[1] Maurice-Francois Rougé, L'age de la géonomie, *Hommes et commerce,* June-July 1955. p. 41.

velopment; then, in what philosophers would describe as a reflexive way, it applied the same analysis and procedure to its own resources. Having seen so many other regions of the world as virgin country, Europe at last learned to look upon itself as a new continent, waiting to be discovered.

From this point of view, the whole world is underdeveloped. *Should the adjective, then, be applied to those countries which make the least use of their exploitable resources? This definition can be used provided two things are kept clearly in mind. First, the idea of what are the exploitable resources is a changing one —in the modern world a rapidly changing one; a few years ago at Chinkolobwe, in the former Belgian Congo, uranium was considered simply as a by-product which had only minor uses and which by itself certainly did not justify working the mine. Secondly, our listing of such possibilities is far from complete; indeed, in the most primitive continents it has hardly been started. Perhaps the most underdeveloped country is the one which does not yet have the most basic equipment, that is to say, the inventory of its own potentialities. To say this is not to deny the theoretical value of the definition, but it lessens its practical value. For who is in a position to make a list of underdeveloped countries based on the criterion of being farthest from making full use of its natural resources?*

Let us next examine the second interpretation of this relativity. Shall we say that an underdeveloped country is one in which the inhabitants do not possess the necessities of life? But the idea of necessity is a very relative one; looked at objectively, is a pair of trousers, or a bicycle, or a refrigerator a necessity? In a hot country the last of those things is the most useful one. In point of fact, it is only in regard to nutrition that the minimum requirements of nature can be ascertained with any degree of precision. A man living in a developed country takes in 3,200 calories daily; it could be said that less than 2,500 signifies an underdeveloped country (the average is less than 2,000 in India, and also in South-East Asia, Asia Minor, and the most backward countries of Latin America, such as Mexico, Central America or Peru). It is still necessary to qualify these purely quantative calorific data with qualitative facts relating to a balanced diet. In general, the diet in underdeveloped countries is unbalanced, the most frequent deficiency being the lack of protein.

Yet these considerations are not sufficient either. Certainly nutrition is of prime importance and Dr. May, Head of the Department of Medical Geography of the American Geographical Society, has made famine maps which more or less coincide with what are usually considered to be the underdeveloped areas. Nevertheless, it is clear that populations may have sufficient food and yet remain at a very primitive stage of intellectual and economic development. For example, the food situation in sub-Saharian Africa, at least in certain regions, is satisfactory, or almost so, yet common sense tells us that Africa is an underdeveloped continent. We see then the criterion of nutrition by itself is inadequate. Yet as soon as we leave the sphere of alimentation, opinions as to what are minimum needs become extremely subjective. Very often, what is necessary means what other people have.

This last remark leads straight to the third interpretation of this relativity. We are no longer comparing the present with the possible, nor reality with necessity; we simply compare the various nations with one another. Underdeveloped countries by general agreement, are those whose economic development has reached only the lowest level and affords their inhabitants only the most elementary standard of living. In other words, an underdeveloped nation can be defined only in relation to a developed nation.[1]

---

[1] This by no means implies that development is a normal state of affairs and that underdevelopment is a kind of pathological atrophy. There is nothing to prove that growth, in the economic and social meaning of the term, is an inevitable or even a likely development for a society *a priori*. "On the contrary," says M. Bertrand de Jouvenel (*The Development of economically backward countries and the problems resulting for France*, lecture given on the 10th January 1957 before the study and liaison committee of the French Union, p. 11) "stagnation is the general rule, and we think otherwise only because we limit our view of history to societies which have undergone development, which have spread abroad their acquired skills and, one after another, have helped to stir up humanity the world over."

But since human societies have been unequally developed since ancient, even prehistoric times, why does the question of under-development receive so much attention nowadays?

The first reason is that for the last few decades this disparity has been much more marked. Moreover, many things have happened to hasten the awareness of this state of affairs among people living in the underdeveloped countries. The most import-ant of these is the sharp increase in the gap between the developed nations of the world and the underdeveloped ones. On the one hand, the underdeveloped countries have been subject to a veritable demographic explosion owing to the rapid fall in mor-tality rates brought about by the medical discoveries made in the advanced countries, with the result that, all other things being equal, income per head has actually decreased in the poorer countries. While this has been happening, the pace of progress in the developed countries has increased considerably. Economic de-velopment is a phenomenon which mathematicians would call exponential, which means that it grows in proportion to itself; the more advanced a country is, the more it will advance. (Just imagine a motor race in which, at any given moment, a car's power of acceleration was proportional to its present speed.) In 1938 per capita incomes for India and America were in the proportion of 1 to 15. Now they have reached a proportion of 1 to 35.

Moreover, it is only comparatively recently that the West has been so far ahead of the other nations in regard to economic development. It is probable that in the seventeenth century the Egyptian fellah had roughly the same standard of living as the French peasant. At the same period, European civilization and Islamic civilization were at comparable stages of development. To go back still further, the Middle East and the Far East have a more ancient civilization than that of Europe. The Pekin Gazette *(China's "Court Circular") is contemporary with Hugh Capet, and we also know that the Chinese had discovered rag paper, printing, the magnetic needle and gunpowder.*

It is only during the last six or seven generations that the West has held the lead, if not over all underdeveloped countries, at least over those just mentioned, whereas it is about 15,000 years or roughly 450 generations since men learnt to polish stone, to domesticate animals, to cultivate plants and to make pottery. Thus the differential between the West and the rest of the world, seen on the scale of human history, is quite a recent event. In a few decades it has reached extraordinary proportions.

There is also the fact that if such large differentials of wealth had arisen between different parts of the world in other ages, they would very soon have been corrected; the inhabitants of the poorer countries would have gone by land or sea in search of wealth, wherever they could find it, just as Europeans took ship for America in the nineteenth century, or, in earlier times, Asiatic tribes conquered Europe and perhaps even peopled South America.[1]

Nowadays, rich nations erect ring-fences around their countries and practise immigration screening specially loaded against the poorer countries, which they consider to be the most dangerous ones. This is obvious in the case of white nations enjoying a high standard of living in territories of excessive size; the United States, Canada and Australia protect their prosperity by stemming the rush of poor immigrants. The only migrations of any size which take place nowadays are the result of specific political situations, owing to which between 1912 and 1950 eighty million people changed their countries of residence.[2]

As for purely economic migration, this is rapidly becoming impossible nowadays. This was brought home to France by two small scale examples. When she tried to persuade some of the inhabitants of Réunion to move to Madagascar or those of the Antilles to Guiana, she met with all sorts of insurmountable diffi-

---

[1] The large movement of Africans to America in the seventeenth and eighteenth centuries can be disregarded because it was involuntary.
[2] Twenty-five per cent of these figures represent populations' movements made compulsory under Hitlerism; one fifth consists of movements of Indians and Pakistani fleeing from one of these countries to the other, after the partition of the Indian Empire. A large, though imprecise fraction represents deportations into Siberia. To this should be added the movement of Arabs when the State of Israel was founded.

culties. *Thus the over-populated nations, unable to do more on a geographical level, have no other resource than to work on a historical one. Being unable to search for wealth where it is, they end up by contriving the means of making it come to them; cut off from the lands where technicians and capital are to be found, they try to make the capital and technicians go to them. Since their ambition can no longer be satisfied in space they place their hopes upon time, and thereupon all these countries re-invent or utilize the idea, which is a very Western one, of time conceived as a progress or development.*

The underdeveloped countries have embraced this decision all the more firmly because various events have high-lighted for them the inequalities which exist among the nations. Not only has the distance between developed and underdeveloped countries increased, it has also become more evident to the latter. It is broadly true that until the last war the existence of economically backward countries did not evoke surprise or incite to action. The great amount of attention now given to the problems of underdevelopment is but a reflection of this recent awakening. Underdevelopment does not really exist until it is known to exist.

Why has our awareness of these problems suddenly increased so rapidly?

The first and obvious cause is the expansion in modern means of information; the press, photography, the radio and the cinema have all been instrumental in bringing the world closer together: western ways of life are known throughout the world and other nations have wanted, more and more, to adopt them.

Moreover, besides the ordinary means of information, we must not forget that unhappy channel of information, the last war; the gigantic struggles which sent armies of foreigners fanning out over benumbed continents, the bloody quarrels of the whites among themselves, the industrial enterprises brought in haste to new countries to meet the requirements of the war, the services which subject peoples were called upon to give and the solemn promises for the after-war years which they obtained in exchange, all these acted upon primitive peoples like an accelerated adolescence.

Thirdly, through chance or destiny, or the weakness of Europe, or for whatever reason, the two most powerful nations in the world are both emancipated peoples. This point is of cardinal importance for two reasons; first of all, it has the force of example, though in fact it is only the Russian example which counts in this respect because it is the much more recent one. Russia has shown that, in a bare quarter of a century, a people can rise from the magma of poor nations to become a first class power. Moreover, both the great powers of the world are very much attached to the idea of emancipation. The United States and Russia are at one in opposing colonialism, and as this is one of the few points on which they agree, there is a spirited rivalry between them in this field.

We have agreed to consider as underdeveloped countries those which are most backward economically and socially. We now have to decide what test of development to apply.[1]

Probably the least inadequate is that of national income per head.

This method has however one practical disadvantage in that the difficulties of measuring national income are greatest in the un-

---

[1] L. M. Sauvy, in his *General Theory of Population* (Vol. 1, pp. 241-2), Mademoiselle Levy, in an article entitled "Criteria of Underdevelopment" in the collective work entitled *Le tiers monde* (p. 139), have enumerated ten or twelve tests of underdevelopment; a high mortality rate, rudimentary hygiene, under-nutrition, small percapita consumption of energy, illiteracy, a high proportion of agriculturalists, under-employment owing to insufficient opportunities of work, inferior status of women, child labour, a small middle-class, authoritarian government of various kinds, the existence of small badly integrated communities and an absence of national unity.

This analysis is interesting although certain parts of it could be disputed; in any case, its object is not to provide practical criteria, if only because all the socio-political elements are necessarily vague. Undoubtedly the most significant of these criteria is the low *per capita* consumption of energy. The figures given by M. Tabah, in an article entitled "The Population of the World and its Raw Material Needs" in *Population* Oct.–Dec. 1953 gives the following figures for energy consumption per inhabitant in 1950, brought to coal equivalent: North America 7,420; Europe 2,990; Oceania 2,860; USSR and certain small countries included with her, 1,780; Africa 200; Latin America 410; Asia 140; the group consisting of North America Northern Europe, Oceania, the USSR and South Africa has an average of 3,660. The rest of the world has an average of 190. The world average is 1,120.

derdeveloped countries because the statistical apparatus is usually weaker there than elsewhere and also, more important, because in primitive economies many activities are outside the money economy, a fact which makes the assessment of values, and even the measurement of quantities, far more difficult.

One theoretical difficulty in this method should also be pointed out; it is by no means certain that the same number of dollars are needed in all countries to purchase the same amount of happiness, even judged by the most material standards. This is obvious if one considers the question of climate. Even as between Strasbourg and Nice, heating and lighting costs differ. Transpose these regional differences to the world scale and they become quite considerable in regard to clothing, housing, and even feeding. Whether I warm myself in the sun or with coal, it is still the sun which is warming me, but in the latter case via the chlorophyllian function of vegetation in the geological eras; yet only the second case is taken into account when national income is being computed. Whether I use sunlight or thermal or hydraulic electricity for light, it is still the same sun which is lighting me, but in the second case either through chlorophyllian assimilation or through the water cycle in nature, again both due to solar energy; yet only the second case is taken into account when national income is being computed.

The goods I receive from nature through the intermediary of other men form part of the exchange economy and will very largely be included in computations of national income. The goods nature gives me through my own efforts, the animals and vegetables which I cause to grow for my own needs, being outside the exchange economy, are harder to include within such statistics. But the goods which nature gives me independently of my own or other people's efforts are necessarily left out of all such calculations, the accuracy of which undoubtedly suffers from this fact.

In spite of these disadvantages, the assessment of per capita national income still seems to offer the best approach to the problem. We now have to decide upon a threshold below which a *country is considered to be underdeveloped. We could place it at approximately two hundred dollars per head per annum.*

On this basis, the underdeveloped countries of the world[1] are those shown as such on the map which follows.[2] Broadly speaking, these are Asia excluding the USSR, Japan and Israel, making 1,400 million people; part of Eastern Europe and certain peripheral countries of Western Europe, making, in all, about a hundred million Europeans; all of Africa except the Union of South Africa, or 200 millions of Africans; continental and insular Latin America except the countries in the Southern tip of South America, making upwards of 150 million Latin Americans; finally, nearly all of Oceania, less Australia and New Zealand, adding a further few million. In all, the underdeveloped part of the world represents between 1,850 and 1,900 million people, or two thirds of the human race.

The most general problems posed by underdeveloped countries thus defined will be examined in the remainder of this book from three points of view successively.

First of all, assuming that a given underdeveloped country has a certain equipment and a certain level of production, does the country provide from this production the greatest possible benefit for the population? Is the distribution of income arising from this production satisfactory? Is there no exploitation? Exploitation by foreign nations which buy the products or by foreign enterprises which take part in their production or sale, exploitation of the producer by landowners, intermediaries, or an excess of population due to lack of instruction and facilities for family limitation?

After problems of income distribution, we shall look at those of development proper. Here we are not concerned with dividing the cake but with making it bigger. What are the means of financing such development through national saving or from abroad? And which methods are best?

---

[1] There are of course underdeveloped regions within countries which are not shown on this list—Southern Italy, for example. It is also true that large parts of the population of a country not classed as underdeveloped may have *per capita* incomes well below 200 dollars.

[2] pp. XX-XXI

Both questions concerning development and those having to do with distribution constantly involve the problem of relations between underdeveloped and industrialized countries. Therefore we must look at the matter finally, not from the point of view of the underdeveloped countries themselves, but from that of the developed nations, and see to what extent the policies of the great powers are involved in it; and this leads us to questions of geo-strategy and geo-politics.

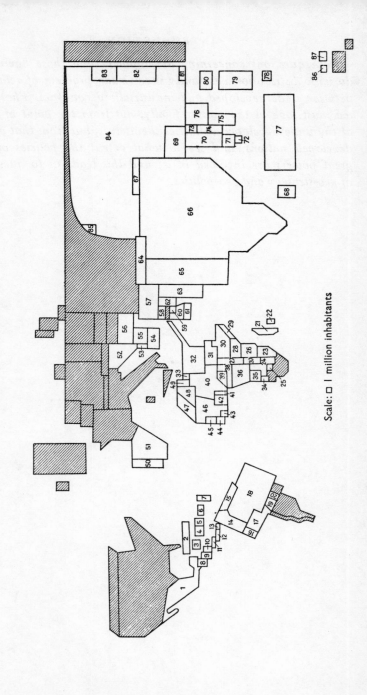

Scale: □ 1 million inhabitants

On the above map the area of a country is proportional not to its territorial extent but to its population. Underdeveloped countries are shown in white, developed and semi-developed ones being shaded.

To avoid excessive subdivision, seven French possessions in East Africa are shown as one, and the four in Equatorial Africa are also amalgamated. Similarly with Bechuanaland, Basutoland and Swaziland.; with Northern and Southern Rhodesia and Nyasaland.; and with the Australian dependencies of Papua and New Guinea. All underdeveloped countries having 1 million or more inhabitants are shown, whether they are independent states or dependent territories. Where a number of states or territories in the same geographical zone have individually less but collectively more than 1 million inhabitants, they have been grouped and shown as one. Such groupings occur among certain islands in Central America (the British, Dutch, and French Antilles, No.7.); Southern Africa (Réunion Mauritius and the Comoro Islands, No. 22.); some West African coastal countries (S.W. Africa, Spanish and Portuguese Guinea, Gambia, No. 34.); various islands or parts of islands off Southern or Eastern Asia (Sarawak, North Borneo, Portuguese Timor, Tyukyu islands, No. 78.); and various islands in Oceania (Dutch New Guinea, Fiji, the Solomon Islands and Hawaii, No. 87.).

1. Mexico
2. Cuba
3. Jamaica
4. Haitii
5. Dominican Republic
6. Puerto Rico
7. Other islands
8. Guatemala
9. Salvador
10. Honduras
11. Nicaragua
12. Costa Rica
13. Panama
14. Colombia
15. Venezuela
16. Ecuador
17. Peru
18. Brazil
19. Bolivia
20. Paraguay
21. Madagascar
22. Various Southern African Islands
23. Mozambique
24. Federation of Rhodesia and Nyasaland
25. Bechuanaland, Basutoland, Swaziland
26. Tanganyika
27. Uganda
28. Kenya
29. Italian Somaliland
30. Ethiopia and Eritrea
31. Sudan
32. United Arab Republic
33. Libya
34. Various West African coastal countries
35. Angola
36. Belgian Congo
37. Ruanda-Urundi
38. Equatorial Africa (formerly French)
39. Cameroons
40. Nigeria
41. Togoland
42. Ghana
43. Liberia
44. Sierra Leone
45. Guinea
46. Ex-French West Africa
47. Morocco
48. Algeria
49. Tunisia
50. Portugal
51. Spain
52. Yugoslavia
53. Albania
54. Greece
55. Bulgaria
56. Roumania
57. Turkey
58. Lebanon
59. Jordan
60. Saudi Arabia
61. Yemen
62. Irak
63. Iran
64. Afghanistan
65. Pakistan
66. India
67. Nepal
68. Ceylon
69. Burma
70. Thailand
71. Malaya
72. Singapore
73. Laos
74. Cambodia
75. South Vietnam
76. North Vietnam
77. Indonesia
78. Other South and East Asian Islands
79. Philippines
80. Formosa
81. Hong Kong
82. South Korea
83. North Korea
84. China
85. Mongolia
86. New Guinea and Papua (Australian dependencies)
87. Other islands in Oceania

Part I

THE EXPLOITATION OF THE POORER NATIONS

Chapter One

IMPOVERISHMENT OF THE HAVE-NOT NATIONS?

AS SELLERS of raw materials in the widest meaning of the term, including foodstuffs, which they exchange for finished products, the underdeveloped countries have a prime interest in the prices of these raw materials—the prices in real terms, that is, meaning the quantity of finished goods which can be purchased for a given quantity of primary products.

Are prices of primary products high enough? Even if we examine each product separately, there is insufficient information available to answer this question categorically. What amounts of cloth, tools or cement ought a ton of groundnuts or cocoa or tin to buy? The only objective standard of comparison is the price yesterday or the day before. Therefore a factual approach to the problem of the prices of primary products involves a study of their fluctuations, whether long term or short term. There are examined in chapters I and II respectively.

First, then, has the trend of terms of trade over the last few decades been favourable or unfavourable to primary producing countries?

Many writers would answer that the trend has been extremely unfavourable. They would base their views on a study published by the United Nations in 1949[1] in which it is stated that between

[1] *Relative prices of exports and imports of underdeveloped countries,* UNO (No. 1949, II, B. 3).

1876 and 1938 the average prices of primary goods fell by approximately a third in relation to those of manufactured goods.[1]

These figures suggest the idea of a *progressive spoliation of the poorer nations*, whose primary products are being sold on increasingly unfavourable terms[2]—Lassalle's brazen law of wages again as it were. What are we to make of this movement of prices? Will it be reversed? Should steps be taken to reverse it?

In judging this movement of prices revealed in the UNO statistics, we need to bear in mind certain observations: first of all, the movement is not general; some products have markedly increased in value during the last hundred years—wood, for instance. Moreover, using the same method as for the period 1876 -1938, we find that the terms of trade were moving in favour of the underdeveloped countries during the first three quarters of the nineteenth century, and again since 1938. It could indeed be replied that what happened a century ago under vastly different economic circumstances from those to today is not very relevant, and that after 1938 the war and its aftermath caused a boom in primary products which could be considered as a temporary phenomenon (has not a new trend in the terms of trade become noticeable since 1950?).

But the following observations are more conclusive. In the UNO statistics the prices of primary products, particularly for the earlier years, are of necessity observed at the point where they can be most readily obtained, namely, at their point of entry into the industrialized countries.[3] But at this point the prices of primary

[1] In the above study two indices are used. In exchange for the export of given volume of primary products, if in 1938 a volume 100 of manufactured goods could be imported, then 60 years earlier, in the period 1876-80, volume 147 (according to one of the indices) or 163 (according to the other one) could have been purchased.

[2] Since exports of basic products by the non-industrialized regions of the world had reached an annual value of 6,500 millions of current dollars in 1937-8, these countries would have been robbed of 47 per cent or 63 per cent of this amount by comparison with 1876 prices. This equals 3-4,000 million 1938 dollars (8-10,000 million of today's dollars, or one and a half times the total value of assistance given annually to the underdeveloped countries; cf. Chapter IX, p. 98 and Chapter X, pp. 109-110).

[3] One of the two sets of statistics used in the UNO report is based entirely on British import and export statistics, and statistics from industrialized countries figure very largely in the other one also.

products are c.i.f. which includes, among other things, the cost of sea freight. Thus a fall in the price of primary products may in part signify a fall in freight charges; in fact, Ellsworth has claimed that for the period from 1876 to 1905 the decline in the prices of primary products in Great Britain is attributable, largely if not wholly, to the considerable fall in freight rates.[1] If this be so, it is conceivable that the terms of trade for the underdeveloped countries may even have improved during those thirty years.

Furthermore, a close examination of the variations in the price index for primary products, particularly in respect of Britain's foreign trade, from 1876 to 1938, reveals that this index is strongly influenced by certain primary goods, especially by wheat. This phenomenon corresponds to the opening up during the period of new major sources of cereal supply—the United States, Canada and the Argentine. Rostow[2] has shown that the notable improvement in Britain's terms of trade between 1873 and 1914 was preponderantly due to movements in two products : the price of coal exports rose[3] whilst lower prices were paid for imported wheat.

The importance of wheat in the above story suggests two observations. First, today's underdeveloped countries are not large wheat producers. Secondly, the fall in the price of wheat during the period in no way depressed the economic situation of the countries on the continent of America, which at that time were underdeveloped. On the contrary, the production and export of grain proved to be a new source of wealth for them; it was the producers in Europe, the developed continent, who were hardest hit by the fall.

Yet notwithstanding the above reservations, it is likely that

---

[1] The terms of trade between primary producing and industrialized countries, *InterAmerican Economic Affairs*, Vol. X, summer 1956.

[2] *The Process of Economic Growth*. Oxford, Clarendon Press, 1953.

[3] The change in coal prices was due partly to the industrial development of Western Europe in the second half of the nineteenth century, which greatly increased the demand for energy, and partly to the improvement in wages in Europe. This improvement was general, but it was particularly noticeable in mining activities where little technical advance was made.

during a part at least of the period under discussion, the value in real terms of many primary products originating in underdeveloped countries have fallen, though this is not so scientifically established as many people declare it to be. This fall may well be largely attributable to special factors, such as those mentioned above with regard to wheat, and it is perhaps unwise to deduce from it the existence of a general law affecting all indigent peoples.

One often hears it said, however, that there is one omnipresent factor tending to depress the prices of primary products, namely the monopolistic organization through which the developed countries impose their prices, both for the purchase of primary goods and for the sale of manufactures. But in truth, with a few exceptions, such a monopolistic organization does not exist. One has only to watch industrialized countries trying to sell equipment to underdeveloped countries and to note how fiercely they compete with one another on prices, on length of credit extended and rates of interest which it carries.

It is over-simplifying the problem to picture on the one side the American or British producer of manufactured goods and on the other, the producer of raw materials in Brazil or Senegal. In reality, the chain of production and exchange has many links; at one end there is the small grower or miner in the underdeveloped countries, and at the other end the worker in the industrialized countries.

The efforts of the workers in industrialized countries to obtain high wages have undoubtedly contributed more than has the profit motive of the industrial or commercial leaders towards a certain deterioration in the terms of trade for the underdeveloped countries. For the wage earners have done their best to acquire for themselves the added value due to technical progress, and they have in large measure succeeded. Had they not succeeded, the industrialists of America and Europe would no doubt have wanted to retain it for their own enrichment, but competition would often have prevented them from doing so. This means that, in so far as the benefits accruing from technical progress remain in the industrial countries, it is largely because the workers prevent them from being exported. Without wishing to push the argument to extremes one could even state that it is often the wage earners in Western countries and the peasants in underdeveloped countries who are the adversaries in the conflict over terms of trade.

How are the terms of trade likely to develop in the future? It would be rash to prophesy. The trend of world prices will depend rather on a variety of special factors affecting the various groups of unfinished or finished products than on any universal tendencies.

Nevertheless, there are nowadays some signs that the underdeveloped countries are beginning to work together. It is possible that the nations which produce raw materials may concert their policies in an effort to stabilize and raise the prices of their products. Industrial workers made use of trade unionism to repudiate the iron law of wages and to falsify prophecies that they would gradually be impoverished : and what is true inside Western nations can also become true in the relations of these nations with the less developed nations. Already, in certain limited areas, a stabilization and improvement of prices for raw materials is noticeable; this is happening in dealings between France and the french-speaking African countries. It is not impossible that in the more or less distant future the underdeveloped countries may combine to exert collective pressure aimed at increasing their incomes, which means the prices of primary products.

Let us look at the matter first from the strictly economic point of view. The industrialized countries are heavily dependent for their supplies of minerals on the underdeveloped countries, and this dependence is likely, if anything, to increase; not only oil, but also iron and aluminium will be obtained increasingly from the new continents.[1]

In regard to vegetable products, however, the position of the

[1] See Chapter X, pp. 109-116

underdeveloped countries is much weaker. To begin with, some of these can be produced in the territory of industrialized countries, either identical products (such as rice or cotton) or their equivalent (sugar beet has partially taken the place of sugar cane; colza is tending partly to replace groundnuts). Moreover, vegetable products meet heavy competition from substitutes; in 1914 these represented only 3 per cent of the raw materials used by industry whereas now they account for 15 per cent.[1]

Thus the ability of underdeveloped countries to make industrialized countries heed their wishes varies a great deal according to the raw materials which they produce. But that is only one aspect of the matter. On the one hand the underdeveloped countries are of interest to developed nations as actual or potential consumers of their own products, which means that stabilization of the prices of primary products at a higher level could give a fillip to the economies of industrialized countries.[2] On the other hand, the "have-not" nations are politically so important nowadays[3] that the industrialized world divided as it is into two hostile *blocs*, cannot lightly incur the hostility of the countries which furnish primary products.

Beyond question, one of the most effective ways of helping them would be to stabilize the prices of their products at a higher level. Exports of basic products by non-industrialized regions of the world amount to about 25 thousand million dollars per year;

---

[1] It is true that both Europe and North America purchase a great number of agricultural products as foodstuffs from other continents; but they come preponderantly from countries of white population which are well developed or relatively so. This applies to wheat and meat and also to wool (though the latter is not quite so vitally necessary.) Many products which come from underdeveloped countries are luxury goods. A high proportion of them are, in a greater or lesser degree, stimulants, such as tobacco, cocoa, coffee, tea, vanilla and perfumed plants. None of them represents a very stable trade, particularly if the instability of the American consumer when presented with a scientific or pseudo-scientific idea is borne in mind. A medical theory had a grave effect on the tobacco market; and coffee and cocoa are just as vulnerable. For the last fifteen years the United States have been voracious consumers of coffee and this commodity is now their largest single import; but they might just as quickly turn away from it, with an effect on Brazil, Colombia, Central America and a large part of black Africa that would be incalculable.
[2] cf. Chapter XV, pp. 175-178.
[3] cf. Chapter XIV.

thus, a revaluation of only 24 per cent would increase the annual income[1] of the "have not" countries by 6,000 million dollars which is the amount now being given from public funds of all kinds to underdeveloped countries.[2]

It would therefore be reasonable for the industrialized nations to aim at a real, if discreet, revaluation in the prices of primary products.

Recalling the resolution which the General Assembly of the United Nations voted in December 1952, in favour of "Financing Economic Development by the Establishment of Just and Stable International Rates of Payment for Raw Materials" M. Tibor Mende very properly writes:[3] "On the national level, of course, the kind of disequilibrium which the United Nations had in mind has generally been corrected by legislation in favour of the most needy sectors of the country's economy. Such legislation was possible because of the existence of a basic national solidarity. But similar measures should be undertaken in the international sphere out of enlightened self-interest, in the hope that the principle of solidarity might be extended beyond national frontiers." Is it vain to hope that this feeling of international solidarity may finally come into being in a world which does gradually progress, however tortuous the path?

Indeed, a closer look at the national solidarity mentioned by M. Mende suggests that it need not be viewed in too idealistic a light. It should be borne in mind that within modern nations the underprivileged most often contrived to better their lot by becoming a force, either in the strictly economic or in the political sphere. What looks from the outside like a unity held together by a spontaneous feeling of oneness, is more often than not a state of equilibrium due at any given moment to the interaction of many different economic and political forces.

It is not impossible that similar factors could also give birth to international solidarity, and that the economic and political im-

---

[1] This means income caused directly by revaluation; as we shall see, such incomes are subject to a multiplier (cf. Chapter III, pp. 38-39).

[2] cf. Chapter IX, p. 97.

[3] *Entre la peur et l'espoir*, p. 171.

portance of the underdeveloped countries could play a decisive role in this process.

However this may be, it is desirable that the industrialized countries should accept with open eyes a reasonable revaluation of commodity prices. Their chance to do this may come if they succeed in working out mechanisms for the stabilization of primary products; for such mechanisms usually include the fixing of reference prices, and the choice of levels for these can be made with the desirability of an overall revaluation in mind.

Moreover, short or medium term fluctuations in raw materials prices give rise to far more acute problems than their long-term evolution; they are the subject of the next chapter.

Chapter Two

JOSEPH'S POLICY

THE BIBLE relates how Egypt owed a long period of prosperity to Joseph, who correctly interpreted the king's dream about the seven fat cattle and the seven lean cattle and was able to arrange for two seven year periods, one of plenty and one of drought, to be evened out by stockpiling. The modern world displays no such wisdom.

The prices of primary products are constantly changing, but they change most violently in times of scarcity and of extreme depression. Thus, between 1929 and 1934 during the world depression the price of coffee fell by 63 per cent, that of cotton by 67 per cent, that of cocoa by 73 per cent, and that of palm oil by 81 per cent, whilst the price of rubber fell by as much as 89 per cent.

But even apart from periods of economic stress, price variations occur on a scale not generally suspected by the man in the street. Take as an example the period 1950-60, when world shortage due to the war had been overcome. If we look at the quarterly price indices for each main primary product, and divide the highest index figure for the period by the lowest one, we get the following results.

The least unstable commodities are cereals : wheat (quotient 1.2 to 1.7 according to the market), barley (1.6), maize (1.6), oats (1.6), rye (1.9); liquid oils: groundnuts (1.6), soya (1.9), wood (1.4 to 1.9); fuels: coal (1.3 to 1.8), petroleum (1.2).

Metals are the most unstable: copper (2.5 to 2.8), lead (1.7 to 2.5), zinc (2 to 3), tin (1.6 to 2.3), nickel (1.8), aluminium (1.8); textile fibres: wool (2 to 3.3), hemp (2.8), cotton (1.4 to 2.4); most foodstuffs of tropical origin: coffee (2), cocoa (2.8), tea (2.1), copra (2.5), palm oil (2), sugar (2).[1]

There is lastly one product which is subject to extraordinary variations—rubber; its quotient varies from 3.8 to 4.1 according to the market.

It will be seen that in general, *commodities originating in underdeveloped countries are the most unstable ones;* this remark is particularly true of foodstuffs. It is instructive to compare the quotients for these with those for cereals on the one hand and tropical products on the other: among the fats, solid oils[2] are more unstable than fluids, which include, besides some typically tropical products such as groundnuts, several important ones which come from wholly or partly industrialized countries, such as colza and cotton.[3] Coal, too, which is still mainly extracted in industrialized countries, is less unstable than metals, a far larger proportion of which are mined in underdeveloped countries. Petroleum is a special case. It is relatively stable although largely produced in underdeveloped countries; but the great oil concerns of the West can almost be said to enjoy what amount to extraterritorial rights. Lastly, the commodity subject to the most extreme variations is typically an underdeveloped country product—rubber.

We have seen the magnitude of these price variations; their rapidity is often just as striking. For instance, the quadrupling of the price of rubber between 1950 and 1960 really took place between the first quarter of 1950 and the first quarter of 1951. In the space of fifteen months (from the first quarter of 1952

---

[1] Only cane produced sugar is regarded as an exotic product.

[2] i.e. those in which the oil is solid or semi-solid at the ordinary temperature of temperate countries; these form the raw material of margarine and also of soap.

[3] The importance of cotton oil as a constituent of foodstuffs in America is well known.

to the second quarter of 1953) the price of zinc on the British market fell by two thirds.

Serious effects on the have-not nations

We shall now see what effect these price fluctuations have on the small grower in the underdeveloped countries. Assuming tentatively that he produces unvarying amounts of a given raw material, his income will vary in accordance with the price of this raw material.

It is true that the prices of other goods and services, as well as primary products, are affected by cyclic variations; it may therefore be asked whether the peasants of indigent countries will not in consequence recoup as buyers of manufactured goods what they lose as sellers of primary products. They will not, because price fluctations will always bear more heavily on prices of raw materials than on those of manufactured goods owing to the greater flexibility of industrial production. For this very reason, such fluctuations affect the *quantity* of manufactured goods produced more than that of raw materials.

Thus, in a falling market primary producers in underdeveloped countries see the value of their sales falling more quickly than that of their purchases, and where the fall is considerable, this situation can become really serious. But a sharp and pronounced rise in the market has its dangers too, for the peasant farmer is apt to dissipate the unexpected windfall on haphazard purchases, or even to create a new artificial need which will make the next period of scarcity still harder to bear.

Nor is this all. It was assumed above that the quantities produced were themselves constant; in reality, however, a fall in price discourages production, with the result that the effect on the price is multiplied by the effect on the quantity produced. This phenomenon can be clearly seen in running operations, but it is no less marked in the case of annual crops. It is also felt to a lesser degree in perennial cultures such as coffee or cocoa. An examination of price index curves and of volume index curves for the various agricultural products in french-speaking countries overseas shows a striking parallel between the two, particularly for the period preceding the massive expansion of public investments by Metropolitan France.[1]

Of course, a drop in production due to a fall in the market may help create the conditions for a later rise, and vice versa; but its immediate effect is to aggravate the drop in the producer's income, and not correct it.

It would of course be inaccurate to think of agriculturalists in underdeveloped countries as producing only the staple commodities of international trade. Most of them also produce foodstuffs. Yet these too follow very closely any fluctuations in the main international products. Thus, in Togoland the price of chickens moved in a short time from 300 to 700 francs c.i.f. in sympathy with quotations for cocoa on the New York commodity exchange.

Moreover, surveys in Black Africa have shown that the volume of domestic foodstuffs produced varies with the volume of exportable commodities produced. Thus the material wellbeing of the farmer in poor countries is influenced in a fourfold way by changes in world markets: by the price of the products he exports, by their volume, by the price of foodstuffs themselves, and lastly by their volume.

Variations in production bring about fluctuations of commercial activity in two ways: first, they affect it in so far as it acts as an agent of export; then import trade also is affected, because the producers' consumption increases or decreases with their income. Industry too feels these disturbances—at least, enterprises working for the local market do, and especially those which depend on budgetary orders. Thus, the entire national revenue of underdeveloped countries, is seriously affected by fluctuations in the price of raw materials.

This widespread economic incidence of market changes has

[1] In fact, if the volume of investment is very large, two factors operate simultaneously on the volume of production—price and the scale of investment. When investment was smaller than it is now, the effect of price was preponderant.

The statistics show that, all other things being equal, a rise of x per cent in price soon results in an increase in production of about x per cent also; thus, elasticity is approximately 1.

financial consequences. To begin with, fiscal receipts rise or fall in a way which is out of proportion to the prices of the country's staple commodities.[1] The same thing happens to national savings, both private and public; being marginal, they are more sensitive than the price of primary products : and because the volume of savings is so variable, it is difficult to formulate development plans covering several years, and even more difficult to carry them out. The need to import expensive equipment from abroad for such plans further aggravates the problem, since a heavy fall in the total value of exports greatly reduces a country's means of making purchases abroad, known to several economists as "capacity to import".[2]

Towards international action?

A "Josephian" policy, consisting in evening out fat years with lean years, can be envisaged both at the level of the producer, and at the national and the international level.

Producers themselves could take quite effective action; they could set up reserves when the market was good, as is done for example by European planters in Africa. They could also cover themselves by forward deals in products suitable for such operations. But action of this kind is not a practical possibility for small growers of limited education.

Action on the national plane is therefore required. No nation can dispense with intervention in the commodity market, but they often do so intermittently, using *ad hoc* measures. When the situation of the growers or in the mines becomes intolerable, resort is had to relief or subsidies. But as far as agriculture at least is concerned, governments tend to intervene more regularly

[1] This disproportion is due to the following causes : taxes levied on profits have a marginal character, whereas taxes assessed on turnover are in principle proportional to the product; but if market quotations fall very low, the government is obliged to arrange for a certain relaxation : also, as we have already seen, price variations are closely followed by changes in the quantity produced, and this affects the revenue from indirect taxes a second time.

[2] Capacity to import is the product of the volume exported and the terms of trade. M. Parizeau (*The problem of internal financing*, in the symposium *Le Tiers Monde*, p. 326), shows the large annual variations in capacity to import of a number of countries. In Malaya, for example, taking 1948 as 100, the figures for 1949-53 are : 95, 191, 240, 165, 131.

and massively. One of the most notable examples of this are the marketing boards of British possessions or former possessions, which buy tropical produce at prices fixed for each contract and stand the losses, or appropriate the profits resulting from the difference between the world price and the rates officially fixed for the contract. Price stabilization funds have been established in the french-speaking countries overseas, based on the British model but with a more flexible formula.[1]

A fund for regulating the market prices of overseas products backed by the French Treasury, enables advances to be made to the stabilization funds. In the same way the Latin American countries, especially Brazil, have governmental organizations to regulate market prices for coffee and, more recently, for cocoa.

These national schemes are the most notable attempts at devising a "Josephian" policy, but a large part of their efficiency is lost because they are not co-ordinated with one another. Take as an example the policy of using buffer stocks to regulate market prices, which is one of the most promising courses of action. Unless a nation happens to control the world market, or a relatively insulated part of the world market,[2] in a particular commodity, any unilateral action it takes will be wasted.

On the international plane, however, very few important agreements of such commodities have been successfully negotiated. Yet hopes of such agreements were high just after the war. The Havana Charter formulates a complete theory about agreements on primary products, and envisaged an international trade organization. As we know, this organization did not come into being; only a provisional committee, the ICCICA,[3] was set up, and still exists.

From time to time the Economic and Social Council of the

---

[1] Stabilization funds do not in general operate on the basis of a fixed contract price; they damp down the effects of world fluctuations, without entirely doing away with them.

[2] The French market for coffee has until now been insulated from the world market by protective customs, duties and quotas; hence the Ivory Coast has been able, together with one or two other African countries, to act effectively in this market through a stocking policy which gave them virtual control.

[3] Interim Co-ordinating Committee for International Commodity Arrangements.

United Nations, the ICCICA and the FAO[1] turn their attention to the problems of stabilization.

The states subscribing to GATT[2] have thought up a special agreement, SACA,[3] which would set out the rules that should govern agreements concerning primary products; this is still under discussion. In fact, these numerous discussions have so far produced tons of documents but little in the way of definite action.

At present, only three primary products are covered by serious international agreements—wheat, sugar and tin. Nor can it be said that these work entirely satisfactorily.

The renewal of the wheat agreement in 1959 was secured only by the concession of a far-reaching modification which greatly diminishes the force of the undertakings given by the importing and exporting countries.[4]

What is the cause of this inability to act? The blame should be placed first on the shortsightedness of both producers and consumers alike. According to whether prices appear to be rising or falling, one or other of these parties considers the moment inappropriate for stabilizing action and either refuses to take part in negotiating, or does so only with the firm intention of avoiding a positive outcome. This is only too well illustrated by

[1] Food and Agriculture Organization of the United Nations.
[2] General Agreement on Tariffs and Trade.
[3] Special Agreement on Commodity Arrangements.
[4] The former wheat agreement contained undertakings by importing and exporting countries regarding the purchase and sale of specified quantities of wheat within a price bracket. All that the new agreement asks of the importing member countries is an undertaking to buy from the exporting members a certain fraction of their total imports of wheat; and although the fraction is a high one, it may represent quite small amounts, or none at all, if the total imports of the partner country are correspondingly low. The exporting countries undertake to supply the quantities called for at the maximum contract price.

The sugar agreement, which in theory is still valid, provides for the imposition of export quotas on the exporting countries; but at the talks held in October 1961 the interested countries were quite unable to reach agreement on these quotas. (The Cubans demanded a considerable increase in their quotas to compensate for the loss of the exceptionally good market which they previously held in the United States). As a result the agreement, though still existing in theory, is in practice a dead letter.

The tin agreement provides for price stabilization through buying and selling operations on the market by a single agency financed by the participating countries; but the USSR, which is not a party to the agreement, was able in 1958 to upset the market by unloading operations to an extent which jeopardized the continuance of the agreement. In 1959 a gentleman's agree-the following incident : in 1947 when wool prices were falling, Australia, New Zealand and South Africa put forward a stabilization plan; then prices rose again, and the three initiating states hastened to withdraw their proposals.

There is a second cause which seems in many instances to play an important part. *Traders in raw materials set out to make profits, based not on a percentage of their turnover but on price differentials.* They regard stabilization as undesirable, and easily persuade themselves that it is impossible and illusory. Since they are the acknowledged experts in their various countries on the raw materials in which they specialize, they find little difficulty in convincing official circles that this is so.

Such influence is very strong in the United States; there is no doubt that, notwithstanding the understanding shown in some quarters of the administration, *the United States are largely responsible for the failure of many conferences concerned with raw materials stabilization.*

This is a strange aberration on the part of the United States, for two reasons.

The West, and particularly the United States, spends fairly

ment was reached between the participating countries and the USSR, but the threat still remains for the future. Moreover, fresh difficulties appeared in 1961; Bolivia refused to ratify the agreement, and its application was therefore suspended.

There is indeed a fourth agreement, on olive oil; but this provides only for co-operation in research and advertising, not for any organization of the market.

As regards coffee, on the other hand, the tendency since 1957 has been to make agreements aimed at a common stocking policy and the limitation of quantities exported. These agreements, however, were only between producing countries, not purchasing ones;[1] in fact, not all the producer countries were signatories.[2] Moreover, they are signed afresh each year, covering a single season, though it is hoped to conclude a real international coffee agreement in 1962.

Of other products it can be said in general that study groups are in being but that no definite organization has yet resulted.

---

[1] Nevertheless France, a large consumer of coffee, played an important part in these talks through her links with the countries of the French Community; and the United States, anxious to help the development of Latin American countries, also used her influence in favour of a successful outcome.

[2] The Mexico (1957) and Washington (1958) agreements were signed only by Latin American producers, but the 1959 Washington agreement was signed in addition by Portugal and the French Community. Belgium and Great Britain did not join in.

considerable sums on aid to underdeveloped countries. Yet it is easy to see that fluctuations in the market prices of staple commodities cause sudden increases or falls in the revenues of underdeveloped countries, which far outweigh those available from investments financed by foreign aid.

For example, in countries such as those of Black Africa, a 50 per cent rise in the prices of primary products will, all other things being equal, cause the value of the national product to rise by about 70 per cent. If, as often happens, a change of this magnitude occurs within a short period, say one year, the effect on the national product is equal to that which would have been produced by investing in the country in one year three times the equivalent of the national product.[1] It is most unlikely that investment has ever been made so intensively in any country.

The variation in national revenue produced by investment is naturally very different from that caused by a change in market prices. Whereas the former is durable, the latter is a chance phenomenon. The object of comparing the two is simply to make the point that by allowing such large variations in the prices of primary products, the industrialized countries are inflicting upon the economies of the poorer nations shocks of a severity which completely dwarfs the growth due to financial aid. It is therefore no exaggeration to say that stabilization is the first duty which the industrialized countries owe to those which produce raw materials, investment taking only second place.

There is a further reason why the West would be well advised to make strenuous efforts to combat fluctuations in raw materials prices. This is that *the USSR will beyond doubt make this question one of the planks in its economic propaganda from now onwards*. Already on a number of occasions the USSR has offered long-term contracts at fixed, or almost fixed, prices. Cotton from the United Arab Republic and rice from Burma are examples, and such offers are certain to become increasingly common.

[1] We shall see in Chapter VII that in Black Africa, an investment of 420 units is needed to raise the national product by 100; hence, a rise of 70 per cent in the national product implies an investment of $70 \times 4.2 =$ approximately 300 per cent of the national product.

This is emphasized by the considerable and sometimes startling growth in trade between the USSR, with its satellites, and the non-Communist underdeveloped countries. Between 1955 and 1957 imports into the USSR from India increased from 18 to 168 million roubles;[1] imports from Indonesia increased from 15 to 79 million roubles; imports from Malaya increased from 15 to 79 million roubles; imports from the United Arab Republic increased from 62 to 466 million roubles, and those from Ghana increased from 46 to 76 million roubles. Exports to these countries from the USSR, also increased markedly; for example, those to India from 29 to 339 million roubles, and to the United Arab Republic from 45 to 347 million roubles. The latter country does 37 per cent of its trade with the Sino-soviet bloc.

If we place these two facts side by side—the expansion of Soviet trade with non-Communist countries, and the systematic use of long-term coutracts at stabilized prices, it becomes clear that the West can afford no further delay in grappling with the problem of regulating market prices.

Far from Stalin's theory of a world divided into two great markets, we shall soon witness a struggle between the two *blocs* for the trade of the third market, that of the underprivileged nations. This competition between the two *blocs* may present these nations with an opportunity such as they had not dared to hope for. We are entitled to hope that the United States, which can make the biggest contribution to world stabilization of raw materials prices, will resolve to meet this major challenge of competitive coexistence.

Given that stabilization may be brought about by competition between the world *blocs* or by the more desirable[2] course of fully international co-operation, which is the method best calculated to succeed?

The most effective means would be a series of agreements by products, containing clauses varying according to the technical and economic factors appropriate to each product. These agree-

---

[1] At the time a rouble was valued at one quarter of a dollar.
[2] See Chapter XVI.

ments would almost inevitably conform to one of the three following types :[1] Multilateral contractual agreements, stating the quantities which the various selling and purchasing states agreed to exchange during a certain period, and setting out the prices at which the commodities should change hands or, in any event, the limits within which these prices could fluctuate; international quota agreements, which indirectly limit the possible price variation by regulating the volume of production, or of imports or exports; or international agreements including a buffer stock, thus indirectly limiting the possible price variation by means of stockpiling purchases or sales from the buffer stocks, these operations being undertaken either by a common agency or by the interested nations in concert.

Undoubtedly the elaboration of such agreements would be attended by formidable technical difficulties, the most serious being of course the choice of the price or prices, both in multilateral contractual agreements and in agreements regarding a buffer stock (since reference prices would have to be settled, above or below which stocks would be diminished or increased). A reasonable attitude on the part of all negotiating parties, especially those whom the trend appears to favour, is essential here. Importing countries should not lose sight of the fact that a reasonable revaluation of primary products supplied by underdeveloped countries is desirable not for those countries alone but also, indirectly, for the importing countries themselves.[2]

The fact is that what is lacking most of all in such negotiations is not technical intelligence but the will to succeed, the absence of which is often camouflaged by so-called technical difficulties; each attempted solution raises another alleged problem : statistics are never good enough, studies never sufficiently thorough, committees give birth to sub-committees which suggest that commissions be set up.

Pending the achievement of *stabilization*, which presupposes a series of agreements by products, it would be beneficial to in-

[1] *Commerce des produits de base et développement economique,* UNO *doc.* E/2519, 1953, (No. 1954, II B. 1) pp. 49-60.
[2] cf. Chapter I and Chapter XV, pp. 175-178.

troduce certain compensatory measures[1] with the object of coun-
teracting the effects of price fluctuations on underdeveloped
countries by the grant of loans. For this purpose too it would still
be necessary to fix a reference price : if sales were effected at a
price lower than the reference price, a loan would be granted
equal in amount to the loss of national revenue occasioned by the
margin between the actual price and the reference price. Repayment would be made on a similar basis, i.e. when the market price
exceeded the reference price. What is here proposed is, in fact,
the transference to the world scale of the mechanism set up in
1955 in the franc area by the creation of a fund to regulate
market prices of overseas produce. This fund, backed by the
French Treasury, makes advances to the various stabilization
funds for the French overseas territories. Incidentally, this would
not necessitate the creation of yet another international organization, since the International Monetary Fund could be entrusted
with the task of making this system work, though the necessary
financial backing would of course have to be given to the IMF.

[1] cf. *Commerce des produits de base et développement économique,* UNO
doc. E/2519, 1953 (No. 1954, II B1) pp. 79-85.

Chapter Three

"FIFTY FIFTY"

WE HAVE discussed in the preceding chapters what quantity of finished products an underdeveloped country should receive in exchange for a given quantity of its own primary products; but it is not enough to know the answer to that question. In many instances the primary products coming from the underdeveloped countries are produced by undertakings where management and capital are provided by nationals of industrialized countries. This gives rise to another problem for countries producing primary products : how is the income arising from the conduct of the undertaking in question to be divided between the host country and the foreign enterprise?

Let us imagine an extreme case in which a given product of the soil, or from the ground, is extracted without giving rise to the payment of any local wages or taxes. In such a case it would be of little interest to the underdeveloped country whose soil or sub-surface contained these riches to know what price this raw material would fetch on the world market, for it would be effectively robbed of the entire revenue arising from the product. Clearly, so extreme a case is purely imaginary; a foreign undertaking operating in an underdeveloped country can avoid neither the payment of a certain share to the state, particularly in the form of taxes, nor some distribution of its income within the state, usually in the form of wages.

Fiscal policy of underdeveloped countries

The traditional way in which companies of foreign origin producing raw materials are made to contribute to the finances of the host country is by taxes levied on the products, whether assessed as they cross the frontier (by export duty, the method most commonly in use except for petroleum) or whether they are imposed at the time of extraction (extraction royalties are frequently used in connection with mining, and particularly for petroleum extraction).[1]

These duties, based upon production, form the backbone of the traditional fiscal system in use in underdeveloped countries in dealing with enterprises of the type we are considering here. The rest of the system consists of duties on materials imported by these concerns and of miscellaneous receipts such as, in mining, duties based on the grant of the concession.

So primitive a tax structure is ill-adapted to the needs of development. First because taxation of the products is in itself economically neutral, and does not encourage local processing.

Secondly because it is rather absurd for a country which wishes to acquire modern equipment to tax the import of producer goods. Furthermore, such an unsophisticated system is incompatible with modern revenue practice. There is a certain blindness in taxing basic products, as a country using this system has to choose between keeping the rate of tax low, which limits the resources of the state and thus hampers public development programmes, and fixing high rates of tax with the risk of frightening off possible investors; a state wishing to retain the fiscal flexibility needed for national development has to make taxation of profits one of its main methods. Let us deal with these three points in turn.

Some underdeveloped countries are already using taxation

---

[1] The export duty has the advantage for the producing company of not affecting stocks held locally.

as an economic lever, particularly to encourage local processing of raw materials. In Mexico, for instance, the taxation of mineral production includes *ad valorem* rates decreasing with the degree to which transformation is carried out locally. In Jamaica the royalty on bauxite is lower if it is to be turned into aluminium within the country. Export duties in Malaya are weighted to favour the local tin smelters. In Guinea, any aluminium which may be produced with the help of alumina from Guinean factories is only subject to the same amount of export duty as would have been levied on the quantity of alumina used to produce it.

Secondly, import duties, which are usually heavy in under-developed countries, are nevertheless often reduced or even entirely waived for businesses in the process of installation. This applies to certain specific raw materials imported by the foreign undertaking for its working requirements,[1] above all to specific technical equipment, since it is obviously better to tax the product than the means of production. The adjective "specific" qualifying the words "raw materials" and "equipment" in the preceding sentences should be emphasized. The list could conceivably be extended to exonerate also the raw materials, fuels and other equipment useful to the enterprise but identical with products in use elsewhere in the country, such as cement, gas, oil or typewriters. But although investors often demand concessions as broad as this, it would not in general be desirable to grant them. Apart from the risk of fraud, it is plain that to remit tax on imported products to this extent creates a dangerous sense of hostility among the nationals of the country. It is not conducive to a country's politico-economic harmony for everybody except foreign concerns to pay import duty on any product in general use.[2]

The third aspect of a modern taxation system for under-developed countries requires longer discussion. A tax levied on

[1] This tax remission is really only temporary since in many cases the raw materials in question will leave the country again, incorporated in a finished or semi-finished product; it is better to tax the goods when they leave the country rather than at entry.

[2] We shall discuss the feeling of hostility to extraterritorial privilege at greater length later on (pp. 35-38).

production takes account of the receipts of an enterprise but not of its expenses, and this can become very inequitable when the tax becomes heavy; it does not leave the business sufficient room to manoeuvre when economic conditions become difficult. Where taxation is heavy—and this cannot be avoided in a country in the throes of modernization—it should take into account, at least in some measure, the expenses of a business as well as its receipts. That is the main argument in favour of levying taxation, in part at least, on profits.

Taxation of profits is desirable for another reason. Under the fiscal legislation of certain capital-exporting countries (for instance the United States and Great Britain) tax on revenue or profits paid in another country is deducted from the income tax payable in these countries whereas other taxes paid abroad are deductible only from the calculation of income tax liability. There is thus a marked trend towards taxation of profits in countries influenced by anglo-saxon, and particularly British, ideas.

The idea of connecting taxation with profits has taken such a firm hold in the underdeveloped countries that it has to some extent permeated the whole of tax legislation. Thus, in the oil world, the formula known as "50-50" has come into being. This means that, taking into account all direct and indirect taxes, the enterprise which is exploiting the country's resources shall pay to the state a sum equalling that which it gains itself from its operations.

This system, which first appeared in 1948 in Venezuela, has spread to the Middle East and also to other Latin-American countries. It is one of the basic concepts in oil legislation throughout the world.[1] The application of this principle naturally entails a decision as to how the net revenue of the undertaking is to be arrived at. This question is more complex in petroleum exploita-

---

[1] In Venezuela fifty-fifty was laid down as the minimum to be paid to the state; if the ordinary taxes do not amount to this figure, additional tax is levied to make up the difference. In other countries this figure is regarded as a maximum, tax being abated if it is exceeded. The two cases are not really so dissimilar as they may at first appear, since in both an equilibrium around 50 per cent is aimed at.

tion than in any other field.[1] Clearly, then, the 50-50 system can cover widely differing realities. Under the same formula, states which have been oil producers for many decades, such as Venezuela and the Middle Eastern countries, have been able to obtain terms which are in reality far more advantageous than can nations whose oil potential is less certain.

The 50-50 formula has been found so attractive that it has been extended beyond the oil world; it has been invoked in the installation of a number of mining projects. In this connection, the agreements between the Republic of Liberia and LAMCO[2] may be mentioned.

Nevertheless, negotiators from producer countries have been alerted, and the main producers have gradually come to demand the revision of the 50-50 formula, notwithstanding the worldwide threat of overproduction. Venezuela has managed to shift the proportions to 60-40. When new agreements are signed on a 50-50 basis they also include "goodwill payments" which may amount to considerable sums, besides giving the state a holding in research and operating companies on very favourable terms.

However, the prestige of the 50-50 formula suffered during the years 1957-60, mainly owing to action taken by certain nations who were in a hurry to acquire sources of supply which they had previously lacked. In negotiations with Saudi Arabia, Japan accepted a less favourable formula (Arabia 57, Japan 43); whilst Italy[3] has even settled for 75-25 in a number of agreements, notably those with Iran and Morocco.

True, the changes covered by the changed formula are not always so great as might be imagined.[4]

[1] In particular, the results can vary a great deal according to the degree of generosity with which the state handles provision for reconstitution of strata.

[2] Liberian, American, Swedish, Minerals Company, which is interested in iron ore deposits in Liberia. 50 per cent of the shares have been issued to the Liberian government, which therefore receives 50 per cent of the distributed profits, free of all taxes.

[3] With Signor Mattei, Chairman of the state-owned "Ente Nazionale Idrocarburi" as the leading spirit.

[4] For example, in the agreement between Italy and Iran, only 50 per cent of the profits are returned as taxes; but an Iranian state-owned enterprise (CNIP, the Iranian National Petroleum Company) will own half the capital once working begins, and in this capacity it will receive half of the profits,

Although this development in the financial system towards taxation of profits is a very necessary one, it is not progressing without setbacks and difficulties. In countries under French influence taxation is still preponderantly based on production; this is seen very clearly in the financial agreements connected with the large projects in Black Africa. The discussions which took place between the petroleum company in Gaboon and the public authorities are very instructive in this respect. They started from the fifty-fifty formula but, in the end, did not adopt it since the local authorities preferred to cut down profit taxation sharply, although later on it might have brought in considerable amounts, in order to obtain the immediate revenue accruing from taxation based on production. There, in a nutshell, is the problem; taxation of profits, which is better adapted to the fluctuations of the market, has for the state the disadvantage of greater uncertainty; particularly where oil is concerned, a financial assessment based on profits associates the state more closely with the risks run by the prospectors. On the other hand, after the initial period the repercussions of market fluctuations are felt more strongly by direct taxes, which have a marginal character, than by indirect taxes.

For a full appreciation of the problem raised by the choice between direct and indirect taxation it is necessary to take into account a new and vitally important fact: the *development*, as regards private investment in the underprivileged countries, *of the idea of consumer co-operatives*. The prospective users of the products produced by such undertakings figure with increasing prominence among the shareholders in Latin America and in Africa. This is due, first of all to the decreasing importance of the finance market in favour of self-financing, and secondly to the

i.e. 25 per cent of total profits before tax. What is original about the scheme is rather the provision that the Iranian state's share of the capital has to be paid, not immediately but by way of sums retained from the profits due to it, the Italian group meanwhile advancing the money. Thus, it really amounts to a loan on which the Italian group receives interest indirectly, since the Iranian government charges no rental for the land which is utilized. One could therefore say that the 75-25 formula, if we look at it closely, is but a variant of 50-50.

difficulty of getting investors to put money into the under-developed countries nowadays. In addition to the bait of the future dividend, an interest in the product itself is often required.

The capital structure of the companies connected with large projects in Black Africa shows how strongly the consumers predominate; first in importance are industrialists using the raw materials in question, and secondly traders specializing in this material. In the iron mines of Mauretania 65 per cent of the capital belongs to French or European consumers.[1]

In the Ogooué Mining Company which will exploit the manganese from Franceville, American and French users own 68 per cent of the capital.[2] In the Mekambo Company prospecting for the iron of the Gaboon, American and European users have 75 per cent of the shares; the Bethlehem Steel Corporation would in fact have preferred it to have been 100 per cent. In the Fria Company in Guinea (bauxite and aluminium) the figure does reach 100 per cent.[3] Here we have the extreme case : the pure user's co-operative or as the Americans call it a "captive company" (being a prisoner of the purchasers of its own products).

The conflict of ideas between users and financiers is very marked nowadays in the world of investment in underdeveloped countries, the rivalry between these two groups being a dominant theme. The users distrust the financiers, not only because industrialists always feel distrust to some extent where finance is concerned, but also for more special reasons. The users think : "We need to see such a project carried through, so we will do it ourselves; we are not speculators; financiers are always more or less speculators." They fear that in pursuing their speculative aims the financiers will not give thorough support to the project. The memory of the Canadian Frobisher Group, a finance company which was an important shareholder in the Mauretania Iron

---

[1] This figure includes the 5 per cent belonging to the Société Denain-Anzin which is not itself industrial but which has close links with USINOR.
[2] This figure includes the share belonging directly or indirectly to Mokta el Hadid, a specialized trading company, amounting to 19 per cent.
[3] The only exception are the agreements signed in 1958 between Péchiney-Ugine, on the one hand, and COFIMER on the other. COFIMER is a finance company.

Mines and which sold its holding even before the prospecting was finished, is still very vivid. Because of such happenings the users have now made doubly sure in projects of this sort by including clauses enabling the existing shareholders to purchase the share of any defaulting shareholder, and in many instances placing very severe limitations on the sale price for such shares.

But what is mainly at stake in the rivalry between the users and financiers is the future financial policy of the company. The financiers are looking for dividends, since they obviously need a generous dividend policy to be able to market their shares to the public. The users, on the other hand, want to pay the lowest possible price for the product, even if this means receiving low dividends; indeed, the ideal for them is to have no dividends at all and a very low price, this being the classical co-operative idea : the aim of a co-operative is to sell its products cheaply to its own members. It might be thought at first sight that these alternatives come to the same thing, but here financial considerations come in again. If the industrialist repatriates his profits he will pay tax on them in his home country, whereas if he simply buys his raw materials more cheaply he will avoid doing so.

Moreover, it is not only taxation in their own country which the users hope to avoid, but also in certain cases taxation in the underdeveloped country too. If they are not careful such countries could well see their taxes on profits falling to a very low yield or even none at all, owing to undervaluation of the product exported. In some respects, then, the interests of the underdeveloped country coincide far more with the financiers' than with those of the users. It is to the advantage both of the host nation and the financiers that the company should make profits by selling at the world price. The industrialists, on the other hand, are interested in seeing the company make no profits by selling at cost price. It is, of course, open to the financial authorities to query the selling prices put forward by the undertaking and to tax them on the basis of the world price. But the concept of a world price is clearer in theory than in practice, and such discussions can therefore become quite complicated, the more so as the company has the advantage over the tax authority of a very thorough knowledge of the technical aspects of production.

Clearly, then, an underdeveloped country has to take into account many different considerations in setting up its system of taxation. Usually it will be best to include both direct and indirect taxation in the system. A good aim in most cases would be to obtain about half of the total tax revenue from company profits, but in the case of a consumers co-operative the yield from this item will obviously be well below that figure. Moreover, when the undertaking is producing a raw material the price of which is comparatively stable, there are fewer disadvantages in basing the tax on the product itself.

Whatever basis an underdeveloped country selects for its taxation it cannot escape a further question which is even more important, both for itself and for the investors. Taking all the taxes together, what will be the total sum which the undertaking has to pay? Clearly there must be an optimum figure for this, below which the state is foolishly throwing away budgetary resources which it badly needs and above which it will frighten off possible investors and kill the goose which lays the golden eggs. This optimum figure naturally varies from case to case. Nevertheless, the concept that in an average year the total tax payable ought to be approximately the same as the net revenue of the investor, at least in respect of undertakings requiring fairly heavy investment, may serve as a rough approximation. Here once more is a 50-50 formula, but only as a point of reference, not as an official basis of taxation. One of the consequences of using this ratio would be that the smaller the amount of money distributed in the underdeveloped country, particularly in the form of wages, the larger would taxation bulk in relation to the turnover of the enterprise. Petroleum companies in the Middle East distribute locally about 20 per cent of the value of their products; the investors' income is around 40 per cent, and total taxation about the same. Taxation amounting to this high proportion of the turnover value could be entertained only by undertakings distributing very little in the way of local wages and salaries. As soon as wages reach a higher level, as is the case with most investments in underdeveloped countries, the tax figure falls to as little as 30 per cent and more often to around 20 per cent of the value of the products.

But the level of total taxation must take account of the special circumstances of each particular case. Desk calculations alone do not furnish a reliable basis; often a search for the optimum levels leads to a bilateral *discussion between the intending investor and the authorities of the underdeveloped country*. The basis on which new enterprises in underdeveloped countries shall be taxed is becoming more and more a matter for individual negotiation. There is nothing necessarily exceptionable in this, so long as this "made to measure" taxation is not carried to excess. If it is, other businesses in the country may get the impression that new undertakings enjoy disproportionate advantages and do not pay their full quota to the general expenses of the nation. One solution which is particularly apt to give rise to this regrettable result occurs when the negotiations result in a taxation formula which excludes common law taxes. It is, on the contrary, desirable that undertakings enjoying a negotiated taxation arrangement should in principle pay common law taxes, and that the negotiations should mainly be concerned either with supplementary taxes or with the way in which existing tax law should be applied to the particular concern. From this point of view current developments in taxing petroleum undertakings are a good thing; there is an increasing tendency to make oil companies pay the ordinary taxes unless specially exempted, and in addition certain special taxes, thus reversing the former system which was favoured in the Middle East particularly, whereby a tax known as a "substitute payment" replaced all common law taxes.

Tax negotiations should not be concerned only with the total amount payable and with the basis of the various taxes. A third concept, that of duration, should be introduced. It is wise for an undertaking to be prepared to bear a higher assessment in exchange for the promise that the authorities will not vary the amount of this deduction for a certain period. Uncertainty about taxation is no doubt felt generally throughout the world; but investors are more fearful when it comes to investing in under-developed countries, because there is a smaller variety of taxable objects in such countries and also because the authorities, being less experienced, are more liable to take sudden and ill-considered decisions. Long-term tax agreements have become one of the basic elements in the development of these countries. Such an undertaking by the authorities can take various forms; it is usually given by the executive, sometimes officially, sometimes unofficially (as, for example, in several Latin American countries). Elsewhere, as for instance in Jamaica, it has a more formal character. In french-speaking countries in Africa long-term taxation agreements are voted upon by the local councils.

Para-fiscal formulas

Taxation is not the only way in which the profits of an undertaking can be shared between its owners and the state; it is simply the most obvious way of doing this but other ways are conceivable.

In the first place, the state could receive part of the profits in the form of a share in the capital, not of a tax. We are not thinking here of the case where the state is an equity shareholder in the company because it has contributed a certain proportion of the initial capital together with the other shareholders, for in such a case the state as such is not deducting anything from the profits of the company : it is one of the co-owners of the company itself. But there are cases where companies grant shares to the state without receiving payment either in money or in kind. Thus in Angola the Government has made an agreement with an oil company renouncing all taxes in exchange for one third of the shares in the company. We saw[1] that LAMCO has given 50 per cent of its shares to the State of Liberia as a substitute for all taxation.[2]

[1] Page 27.
[2] This solution somewhat resembles that in Chile; the state receives 55 per cent of the profits of the Corporation for the sale of Nitrates and Iodine, which has a selling monopoly and is exempt from all taxes.

A state may participate in a company, not free of charge, but outside the ordinary provisions of common law; thus the state may claim the right to purchase the shares of a company at a later date, for example when research is ended and exploitation begins. There are examples of this kind in Iran; in the former Belgian Congo the public authorities reserved to themselves the right to subscribe up to 20 per cent of the initial capital in mining enterprises. Clearly, the possibility of buying shares in a company when it has been in existence and working for several years is a considerable advantage. In turn, the company gains favours of various kinds, especially as regards taxation.

Such formulas have their uses. It may seem to make little difference whether the Treasury receives a certain percentage of the profits in the form of taxation or of a dividend. But the difference is not a financial one. There is an obvious interest in associating natives of the country at management level in the company, which can be conveniently done by nominating one or more members to the board. As would be expected, the contribution made by these people in the beginning is often quite small; but they gradually become familiar with the problems facing the undertaking, in which they feel they have a proprietary interest.

Just as the state may accept a part of the equity in lieu of all or some of its fiscal rights, it may also elect to take delivery of part of the product of the enterprise instead of taxes; in this event the state obtains money by itself selling this part of the product. Thus during several years since 1951, Chile has made the companies producing copper deliver a part of their production at a fixed price to the Central Bank, which in its turn has sold this at market prices; it has been bought, either by the American Government or by private companies, including the copper-producing companies in Chile themselves. The latter have thus bought back their own product at a loss—a fairly thinly disguised form of taxation. Like taxation itself, this method brings money into the Treasury and it also gives the state some control over market prices, besides enabling it to make priority deliveries if necessary to factories working for the nation.

Here is a third example of a para-fiscal mechanism. In Guinea the Société Fria and Les Bauxites du Midi had to agree, in addition to paying their share of taxation, to contribute money to a regional development fund used for carrying out public works. Similarly, in Jamaica, the mining companies were obliged to keep under cultivation land which they had acquired as reserves, and also to hand back land on which mining operations had ceased in a condition fit for agricultural use or, failing this, an equivalent amount of land elsewhere. The latter obligation could be met by the payment of suitable compensation.

In all the cases just cited, the formulas which were developed, apart from taxation in the strict sense, are each of interest inasmuch as they go further than taxation in ensuring a certain interpenetration between the enterprise and the nation, either in giving the nation an interest in the management of the enterprise, or in the sale of its products, or in giving the enterprise an interest in the overall problems inherent in the national development. This advantage may make up for the comparative unwieldiness of such formulas as compared with simple taxation.

On the other hand, no para-fiscal system of contributions should be employed in which this unwieldiness is not balanced by such advantages. The use which some Latin American countries make of foreign exchange operations to obtain hidden contributions from companies is not an example to be recommended : from the foreign exchange earned on their exports, these companies buy the national currency they need for their local expenses, but at a rate considerably less favourable than the rates used for the other requirements of the national economy. In certain years this form of exchange deduction has yielded more than half the total paid on tin operations in Bolivia and more than one third of the total deductions from copper companies in Chile. To obtain forced contributions from necessary local purchases, thus encouraging the companies to seek their supplies outside the national frontiers, is to accentuate the extra-territorial character which foreign undertakings are always liable to have in underdeveloped countries.

Risk of Extra-Territoriality and the Dualist Theory

Taxation and para-fiscal measures are the means by which the State obtains its share of the revenue of foreign undertakings. But this is only a part of a larger question : what fraction of the total revenue represented by the turnover of the undertaking goes abroad? What fraction remains within the country not only in the form of taxation, but also in other forms, especially that of wages?

Almost inevitably a high proportion of the takings of the enterprise leaves the country; this is particularly true of mining and industrial undertakings. An underdeveloped country can usually obtain technicians, patents, equipment and capital only from outside its own frontiers. But each of these four elements implies the export of a considerable part of the revenue of the undertaking.

In many underdeveloped countries it is impossible to find locally not only a manager or an engineer, but even foremen or skilled workers. So they have to be brought in from outside; they require high rates of pay and they nearly always aim to save as much as they can as quickly as possible and to invest their savings in their country of origin. This means that a high proportion of the wages and salaries will leave the country.

Payment for patents and licences often represents a not inconsiderable sum, but taken as a whole it accounts for less than the other three.

Purchases of equipment are covered by the initial capital, so that it could be said that the effect of these two items is not cumulative; nevertheless it should not be forgotten that most undertakings must make provision for industrial amortization and the renewal of equipment, as well as financial amortization.

But the largest payments are those due to the investment itself. Large sums leave the country in the form of capital amortization, in interest and in dividends. Such expenses are particularly heavy in underdeveloped countries in which equipment costs more than in developed countries, and they reach their maximum in projects that require heavy initial expenses. Thus the major concerns of Black Africa (Miferma, Comilog, Fria, Bauxites du Midi, Konkouré, Kouilou) involve total investments amounting to several times the anticipated turnover (from 2.5 to nearly 7 times or from 3 to 5 times overall); assuming a project to be financed as to one third by capital and as to two thirds by loans at 8 per cent repayable in 20 years, and assuming that the average dividend paid is 15 per cent it will be seen that during the first 20 years the total outgoings both to the equity holders and in loan repayments and interest will exceed 10 per cent of the sums invested; if the investment is three, four or five times the turnover the cost of financing the company will, by itself, exceed 30, 40 or 50 per cent respectively of the turnover.

In view of these facts it is not surprising that a large proportion of the income accruing to an enterprise, at least in the field of mining and other heavily capitalized industries, goes abroad and only a small fraction remains in the country in the form of wages or taxes. Detailed estimates were prepared in the case of the nickel industry in New Caledonia, the aluminium industry in Guinea and the iron industry in Mauretania, and these showed that on the average only 29 per cent of the turnover figure for the various undertakings would remain within the country.

This leads the underdeveloped countries to feel that they are being robbed, and that the riches with which nature has endowed them are being exploited without much being left over for them. This situation is represented in economic theory by the so-called *dualist* thesis according to which a foreign undertaking in an underdeveloped country is like a modern oasis in the middle of a primitive desert. Economists who have studied the development of countries in Latin America on behalf of ECLA[1] have underlined the dualist nature of underdeveloped countries in their initial stages.

These studies shed much light on the problems of underdeveloped countries. Undoubtedly one of the dangers facing such countries is to find themselves divided up into a traditional part

[1] Economic Commission for Latin America, a regional organization of the United Nations. See especially the publication of the ECLA No. E/CN12/221 of the 18th May 1951.

which remains primitive and a modern sector which remains *foreign* in the full meaning of the term. Two practical consequences should be drawn from this analysis.

On the one hand, in countries which become partly modernized, owing to the entry of finance and personnel from abroad, it is all the more essential that the rest of the country should undergo an accelerated development and systematic modernization with the aid of public investment from national and international sources. If the modern enterprise is a plantation or an agricultural-cum-industrial complex this aim can be attained in part by a wide diffusion around the undertaking of the cultural technique it is itself using; the agricultural side of the undertaking has a pilot role; if there is an industrial side, this enables it to stabilize prices for the produce of the small agricultural undertakings in the district.[1]

On the other hand, no opportunity should be lost of integrating the foreign enterprise with the host country, whose nationals should be given an interest in the undertaking in every possible way: through financial participation by indigenous persons, whether physical or legal, or by the state itself, and by a public relations attitude and activity adapted to the underdeveloped country.

Notwithstanding the theoretical interest of the dualist thesis, and the important practical consequences which can be drawn from it, its importance should not be exaggerated. There has been a tendency in recent years to let the theory rather overshadow the reality in this respect. For instance, the statement that the great mining projects or industrial projects in Black Africa leave a bare 30 per cent of their turnover in the countries concerned refers to direct revenues. But these incomes are spent by those who receive them, thus creating secondary incomes which in their turn are spent and create tertiary incomes and so on. Even though at each stage part of the demand calls for imported products, another

---

[1] This technique has been adopted in the Mahavavy region of Madagascar around the agricultural and industrial complex of the Mahavavy sugar company (SOSUMAV) which comprises ten plantations and a sugar factory and a refinery.

part, larger or smaller, calls for products supplied by local agriculture or industry, and furthermore even imported products have to be unloaded, transported and distributed, all of which gives rise to incomes in the country itself. Assuming that a constant proportion of the income is spent abroad at each stage, the sum of the incomes generated in the country would appear as a decreasing geometric progression. This means that the total of internal incomes generated by the undertaking is then a certain multiple of the primary incomes. Thus in Black Africa it has been calculated on an average that the total incomes were equal to 3.2 times the primary incomes.[1] Moreover, the multiplier does not affect only the wages distributed; it also acts upon the product of the taxes which are paid, in so far as these are judiciously employed. It thus becomes evident that in estimating the effect of a mining, agricultural or industrial project account should be taken not only of the receipts of the state from taxation and para-fiscal measures, nor even of the total of the revenue accruing directly to the nation, but in addition of the multiplier effect brought into play by the economic context of the country, improved it may be by subsidiary operations.

[1] If we imagine a mining company leaving within the country only about 30 per cent of its turnover, as mentioned above, then owing to the multiplier effect the addition to national incomes will nevertheless amount to something like the turnover figure itself (30 times 3.2 equals 96).

Chapter Four

AGRARIAN REFORM

IN THE three previous chapters we have looked at the problems that occur in the relations of a nation which produces raw materials with other nations, in so far as these buy the raw materials or finance or organize their production. This Chapter is concerned with the underdeveloped nation itself and with the distribution of national income, be its level what it may.

Is the share taken by producers, and in particular by peasants, sufficient? In many cases it is not. The share is excessively reduced by large landowners, middlemen and by the peasant's own prolific offspring. Chapters IV, V and VI deal with these subjects in turn, the present chapter being concerned with the agrarian question.

The existence of an agrarian problem—one, that is to say, having to do with the structure of ownership and exploitation of the land, is characteristic of underdeveloped countries.

With few exceptions, developed countries do not have this problem. In the first place, such countries have generally reached a state of high agricultural production, the largest yields per head coming in countries of the North American or Australasian type whilst the largest yield per acre comes from Western Europe. Then also, where industry plays a fairly or even a very important part in the national economy the division of land is not such a vital question, because land is not then the sole source of incomes. Moreover, the developed countries of the North American and Australasian zones have been peopled only recently, the previous inhabitants having in large measure disappeared or in any case no longer constituting an important part of the land economy. In consequence, the whole agrarian structure is based on recent colonization featuring many medium-sized holdings and virtually without any feudal or quasi-feudal relationships. The countries of Western Europe have had their agricultural crises, some of them violent, but in general these have been resolved, most of them during the nineteenth century, though sometimes earlier and sometimes later, as for instance in Western France, of which it could be said that the agrarian question was not really solved until the law of 1945 and the enactment on tenant farming. Developed countries have agricultural problems, not agrarian ones; they relate to technical matters—the organization of markets, or equipment, agricultural policy as a whole tending to ensure the consolidation of that class of working owners which already predominates.[1]

In underdeveloped countries, on the other hand, the soil is usually almost the only source of wealth, to which may be added in certain cases underground wealth. Moreover, as soon as there is a large population, there is a tendency to exhaust the soil by over-cultivation and so the problem is made worse by diminishing returns. Secondly, the countries in question are very backward by Western European standards and very few of them have undergone, or at least, had undergone immediately after the Second World War, the equivalent of the European agrarian reforms. And besides lacking what may be called the "historical legacy" which Western Europe has, they also lack the "geographical legacy" which North America and Australasia have; that is to say, they do not have large unused open spaces, characteristic of the United States, Canada or Australia. On the contrary, in many of these countries successive layers of population

---

[1] The Soviet Union, which carried through an agrarian revolution during the first half of the twentieth century and chose a structure of land ownership completely opposed to that of other developed countries, is obviously an exception.

have been superimposed, and this has multiplied agrarian problems. In many cases European invasions have complicated the problem, either because Europeans have appropriated the land as in Peru, where the landed proprietor is still the white as opposed to the Indian, or in North Africa with its agrarian problems, or because the Europeans have used their power to maintain pre-existent wrongs, as was quite clearly done by the British in the Indian sub-continent.

Nevertheless, agrarian problems are not the general rule in underdeveloped countries; for instance, in Asia, Laos and Cambodia do not have serious agrarian problems for theirs is a system of small proprietors. But the only large underdeveloped area which has virtually no agrarian problem is tropical Africa. How has the difficulty been avoided here?

The first reason is that, in general, the area has been peopled very thinly indeed by Europeans, principally on account of its climate;[1] thus a whole category of agrarian problems, namely those arising from the contact between the native races and Europeans, does not arise. The second reason is that tropical Africa is relatively thinly populated; this weak demographic pressure explains why an agrarian system and methods of culture are retained in Africa which have long since been abandoned in other underdeveloped continents—extensive culture, crop rotation including long fallow periods, thin cultivation and communal land law.[2]

[1] Europeans have preferred the more hospitable latitudes of Mediterranean or South Africa or countries of low latitude but with compensating altitude in Latin America. Where altitude creates more agreeable living conditions in tropical Africa, as in certain countries of East Africa, the whites form a larger proportion of the population and agrarian problems can arise, even in the violent form of Mau Mau. In the same way, Madagascar, which has a milder climate that that of Black Africa, is the only country in the French community to have agrarian problems which arise from the occupation by European companies of vast stretches of land.

[2] If demographic pressure had been stronger, not only thin cultivation but also collective tenure would have been abandoned. Hard times would have led to the fragmentation of ownership, and each family would then have struggled to make a living on the share of land allotted to it. In the course of a few generations, unequal opportunities and abilities would by a comulative process have created the same problems as exist in other underdeveloped countries.

It would be roughly true to say that the first form of the problem is found in Mediterranean and Eastern Europe and in Latin America. In those countries, there exist side by side with poor families each crowded on to an acre or so of land, great estates which are grossly underfarmed, or which are even uncultivated either because they are used for hunting or pleasure or because they are simply neglected.

The second form is found mainly in Asia, with the large estate swallowing up the smallholding and overtaxing it. Sometimes the landowner exercises certain functions; he may for instance supply working capital : but even then his excessive power enables him to charge exorbitant rents and makes for an almost complete absence of security of tenure. Most commonly, however, the situation is even worse than this. The landowner's services amount to little or nothing, all he supplies being the bare ground. He usually levies heavy tithes which are then spent on non-agricultural pursuits; at best, they are used to buy more property rather than to provide working capital for land already owned, and this increases the price of land and makes matters worse than they were before. Often, however, the product of the tithes is spent outside the country—the well-known figure of the absentee landlord living in luxury in a developed country on the rents from his property in an underdeveloped one. What is more, being absent himself he finds it necessary to employ an intermediary who gradually becomes an oppressor in his turn and takes part of the ground rents for himself. This was the almost universal situation in the continent of Asia as recently as fifteen years ago.

Unequal Pace of Agrarian Reform throughout the World

During the last ten years there has taken place in the underdeveloped countries a tremendous redistribution of landed property, probably affecting more than 250 million acres, or twice the area of France. But the pace has been very unequal in different parts of the world. It has been fast in both Communist and non-Communist Asia, very fast in Eastern Europe, and slow (with some exceptions) in the Mediterranean Basin and Latin America.

The problem was undoubtedly most acute in Asia. With few exceptions,[1] land was already in short supply everywhere and the population was rising rapidly. Land hunger led to an excess of tenant farming and to all kinds of monetary impositions on the producers, especially by absentee landlords.[2]

In pre-revolutionary China[3] tenant farmers usually had to pay 40 to 60 per cent of their harvest as rent, although the landowner supplied only the bare ground. In some regions rents were collected by secondary ground landlords interposed between the real landowner and the peasant and these too collected a tithe for their own benefit. Round about the year 1946, agrarian reform was carried through empirically as the Communist armies advanced, legalization coming later through a law passed in 1950. A great deal of land was redistributed; out of 250 million acres of land cultivated in China towards 1950, 120 million acres were confiscated and distributed to 70 million families.

The main target in India was the system of zamindars.[4] The aim of the reform was to give agriculturalists effective ownership of their land and enable them to pay their dues directly to the state. At the end of the Second World War, 43 per cent of India's cultivable land was administered under the zamindari system; by 1956 this had fallen to 8.5 per cent, indicating that some tens of millions of acres were affected by the reform.[5]

The drive towards agrarian reform has been considerable in many other Asian countries, even excluding Japan with its far-

[1] In Borneo and the Philippines there is still some land available.
[2] This does not apply to countries such as Laos, Cambodia, or Malaya, where the small farmers own their land.
[3] See Dumont: *Révolution dans les campagnes chinoises.*
[4] Under this system, rent collection is in the hands of tax collectors known as zamindars to whom the British administration had farmed out the collection of dues from farmers occupying the land at the end of the eighteenth and the beginning of the nineteenth centuries. These zamindars gradually became a feudal class supplemented by sub-feudal intermediaries between them and the agriculturalists.
[5] Apart from official action, much land has been spontaneously distributed to landless peasants by landowners through the so-called Bhoodan Yagna (land gift) movement, about 3.7 million acres having changed hands in this way so far.

reaching land reform of 1947, since Japan is not strictly speaking an underdeveloped country. By a law of 1953, Formosa partially expropriated the largest estates, affecting, it is said, 71 per cent of the country's land surface. A very large redistribution of land took place in North Vietnam from which eight million agricultural workers benefited. In South Vietnam, although the Americans wanted to promote agrarian reform, hardly anything has yet been done except that when the landowners retired to the towns during the war in Indo-China, those who formerly were farming the land became *de facto* owners, so that when the old owners returned there were negotiations which generally resulted in more favourable tenant-farming agreements.

In South Vietnam, the government has used a large part of the aid received from France in buying back most of the rice-plantations which belonged to French citizens. Various measures, some of them on a large scale, have been taken in Thailand, Burma and Pakistan. It can therefore be said that on the whole throughout both Communist and non-Communist Asia, excepting the Middle East, real though unequal efforts have been made, in some cases with striking results.

Whereas the problem in Asia was to free smallholdings from feudal imposts which were crushing them, in Eastern Europe it was to divide up the large estates. Even after the first world war part of the large landowners' estates had been made over to small farmers in several countries of Eastern Europe. But since 1945 under pressure from Communism large private landed estates have completely disappeared, either by distribution to poor peasants and agricultural workers or by the creation of producers' co-operatives. Several millions of acres have been affected in every country of Eastern Europe.

In Mediterranean countries the agrarian reform movement has not taken such a hold. The population there is of course far less densely crowded than in Asia—in fact, it might be said that Mediterranean peoples would have enough land, if they had enough water. But this land, which in theory would just about suffice, is as a rule distributed with extreme inequality.

The Middle East as a whole is characterized by large land holdings and rack-rented tenant farmers.[1] Agrarian reforms have been carried through in Turkey, the United Arab Republic[2] in Irak (1959)[1] and quite recently in Iran (1961).

What of reform in Southern Europe, with her poor land, over-population and lack of industry, her latifundia? There has been but little in Spain, though a National Institute of Agricultural Colonization has acquired a fairly large amount of land with the object of distributing it to farmers. Still less has happened in Portugal. In Italy, where in 1950 the Senate refused to pass a bill which would have reformed the system of land tenure throughout the country, a considerable amount of land has never-theless been redistributed in the south (mezzogiorno).

Lastly, in Latin America where the agrarian structure is based, with a few exceptions,[3] on vast estates together with a great num-ber of very small holdings, very few reforms have been carried out since the Second World War. Some steps were taken in Guate-mala, but without success, and also in Colombia. Bolivia, by a decree of 1953, has expropriated the large landowners and distri-buted the land to small agriculturalists who had either no land or too little. More recently in Cuba, after Fidel Castro came to power, a far-reaching agrarian reform was instituted. It was characterized mainly by the expropriation of landowners with holdings in excess of a certain size, and of enemies of the régime.

[1] Israel, where the land largely belongs to the State or to a publicly owned company, the Jewish National Fund, is an exception; there, land is rented to farmers. In Jordan, certain parts of Lebanon and Turkey, on the other hand, there are small working landowners.

[2] In Egypt, where 2,000 landed proprietors owned a quarter of the culti-vable area, a decree of September 1952 set in motion an agrarian reform in which some 500,000 acres were redistributed whilst at the same time maximum levels for farming rents were officially laid down.

[3] There are some smallholdings in Colombia, and in Southern Brazil there are some public estates which have been state property since the end of the nineteenth century or the beginning of the twentieth. But only two coun-tries are exceptions from the above agrarian situation in their entirety. These are Haiti, where land has been State property since the beginning of the nineteenth century, and Mexico since the revolution of 1910, itself caused by the revolt of the peasants against the excesses of the latifundia owners. In 1940, about half the cultivated land had been re-distributed and Mexico can thus be said to have carried through an agrarian reform before the second world war.

Both Cuban landowners and a very large proportion of foreigners, especially Americans, were affected by this reform. In other Latin American countries hardly any reforms worthy of mention have taken place. At present, 59 per cent of the cultivable land in Brazil, 65 per cent in Ecuador and 74 per cent in Chile is in the hands of estate owners holding more than 1,000 acres each.

Difficulties involved in Reforms

It is undeniable that far-reaching agrarian reforms are needed in most underdeveloped countries. But the task is not easy, as will be apparent from a consideration either of the means to be used or of the situation created, and the new problems raised, by the reforms when completed.

As to the means, the choice is between the Chinese and the Indian approaches, the former violent, the latter non-violent. Those who reject violence, terror, the horror of massacres and the lasting social trauma resulting from their use in a country, must understand clearly that the other way will take a long time and cost a great deal of money.

Peaceful reforms are almost bound to be long-drawn-out. The landowners fight back and, if it comes to legal action, they are better equipped for litigation than their opponents. Moreover, traditional law is based upon respect for property, and for this reason ordinary courts have an instinctive bias in favour of property-owners—so much so that the United Nations made the discreet suggestion : "In certain circumstances this procedure may perhaps be more effective if it is independent of the general judicial and administrative apparatus."[1]

Again, if it is desired to avoid mulcting the landowners, reform is expensive. As those who are acquiring the land are poor, there is little alternative to saddling the state with the costs of compensation, yet this inevitably entails a grave risk of inflation.

Assuming that the reform has been carried through, the resul-

[1] *Progrès de la réforme agraire,* UNO doc. E/2526, 1954 (No. 1954 II B. 3) p. 349.

tant dangers must still cause the government continued anxiety.

One particular danger arises when estates are divided up and may in consequence be less amenable to modern equipment and techniques of husbandry. Parcelling always raises considerable obstacles, physical and psychological, to the adoption of the most productive methods and equipment.

The second danger is more widespread, and affects any country which adopts agrarian reform, whatever the details of the programme. It is well known that the proportion of income spent on food varies inversely with the size of the income—a common sense observation known to economists as Engel's law. Since agrarian reform always has the effect of transferring income from a richer to a poorer person, the fraction of this income spent on food will tend to increase. As the farmer usually produces, or at all events can produce, edible produce, a large part of his activity will be devoted to producing foodstuffs for his own use. This risk is most acute in the least developed countries where peasants often go hungry. In such countries food consumption shows great elasticity.

But if the peasant eats more, the cities are threatened with hunger. Monsieur Sauvy has pointed out that the first famines in the Soviet Union were not necessarily due to sabotage, but may have been largely the simple and almost arithmetical result of the fact that the Russian peasant was eating more.[1]

The risk is increased if the peasant takes to cattle raising and becomes a consumer of animal products, owing to the wastage of calories inherent in the interposition of an animal process between the vegetal process and man.

Furthermore, if the countryman eats better national savings may well suffer. The large landowner, it is true, spent much of his income on luxuries, and even when he did save, often did so in order to accumulate capital abroad or to invest at home in luxury or speculative projects. Modern governments should have the courage to appropriate the whole or part of the income which the

[1] *Théorie générale de la population*, Vol. I, p. 247.

large landowner used to pocket, and to use it not for the good of the peasantry alone but for the benefit of the community, which could use these resources for investments indispensable to the development of the country. Too often, however, the government lacks the necessary courage, possibly because it depends upon support from the masses and must in consequence give them some immediate satisfactions.

The difficulties and risks of agrarian reform are so great that some people doubt whether they are worth while. But in the majority of cases they are still vitally necessary, even though by themselves they are not enough. They should be but one element of a more thorough-going transformation of the nation, and they also postulate help from outside.

In order to combat the dangers enumerated above, there needs to be set up within the underdeveloped nation a complete system of co-operatives. This is what is done in the Communist world, where the policy has been developed as far as the creation of kolkhozes.[1] In the non-Communist world, where sentiment is strongly against the creation of producers' co-operatives, it is all the more important to set up other forms of co-operatives. We shall return to this in the next chapter.

It is also desirable not to separate agrarian reform from the non-agricultural aspects of national development. It appears that in Formosa the large landowners received blocked compensation which could be re-used in the country's industry. The writer has no means of judging with what success the policy has been applied in this particular case, but the general comment may be made that such methods, the effect of which is partially to transform agrarian capital into industrial capital, can play a useful part

[1] The people's republics lost no time in linking their agricultural reforms with the rapid introduction of a very ambitious system of co-operatives, just as the USSR had done a quarter of a century before. This caused serious difficulties with populations which were quite unprepared for them. China has gone ahead in an extremely progressive way, trying to turn the Chinese peasant who is very strongly attached to private property into "a socialist without knowing it." Provisional mutual assistance groups were set up, then permanent ones, then agricultural producers' co-operatives, and finally full co-operatives; and in 1955 pressure towards the creation of kolkhozes was intensified.

both in lightening the burden of reform and also in associating it in the popular mind with a dynamic attitude to the nation's economy.

To sum up, such a delicate and complex policy can be steered through the various risks and perils enumerated above only by a strong government, able both to guide the producers towards co-operation and the surplus of incomes towards investment. Of all the problems with which a developing country is faced, agrarian reform is perhaps the one which calls most insistently for compliance with certain basic rules of political psychology, which will be dealt with in Chapter XIII.

But inevitably, in this field as in so many others, the strong government which is needed is bound to degenerate into a violent tyranny unless the difficulties it encounters are alleviated by help from outside. It would seem that one of the most worthwhile objectives which developed countries could have in giving financial aid to underdeveloped ones would be the international financing of agrarian reform.[1]

[1] cf. *Rapport sur un fonds spécial des Nations Unies pour le développe ment économique* UNO doc. E/2381, 1953 (No. 1953, II B. 1) p. 3.

Chapter Five

FROM MIDDLEMAN TO CO-OPERATIVE

BESIDES THE debt with which their land is encumbered, the peasants of underdeveloped countries have to carry the burden of middlemen.

Supposing that the world price of a certain raw material is known, and also freight charges, we can find the f.o.b. price obtainable at the port of shipment. But to work back from there and find the price the grower will receive, we must subtract first the merchant's cut, then the remuneration of the carrier and of all the other aides along the line, not to mention taxes. An idea of the proportion going to all these auxiliaries can be gained by considering as an example the African countries in the French community.

Table 1 overleaf gives the f.o.b. price and the average price[1] to the grower of the four main commodities produced in the 1957-58 season, in metropolitan Francs and in kilogrammes. But the producer is also a consumer. Many middlemen (in general, the same ones) stand between imported merchandize and the consumer up country. In table 2 overleaf follows some further examples, also from Black Africa, covering recent years concerning four important consumer products (in metropolitan francs).

Thus the peasant has to pay very heavy middlemen's charges

[1] The further he is from the port of shipment the less the grower receives; the figures shown apply to medium distances.

TABLE 1

	Groundnuts (decorticated)[1]	Cocoa[2]	Coffee[4]	Cotton (fibres)[3]
c.i.f price	98.50	356	372	334.50
f.o.b. price	90.40	338	353	320
Price to grower :				
Stripped at weighing machine	74.80	150	272	
Up country (average) . .	73	140	262	159
Difference between f.o.b. price and up country price . .	17.40	198	91	161
Of which :				
Local taxes	13.80	44	32	30
And amounts payable to stabilization fund . . .		+61	+20	+37

TABLE 2

	f.o.b.	c.i.f.	Retail price
Lump sugar (Kg) . . .	92	102[4]	240[5]
Storm lanterns (each) . .	140	198[6]	500 to 900[7]
Tennis shoes[8] (pair) . .	284	340[6]	550[9]
Printed cotton loincloths (each)	966	1034[6]	2000 to 3400[10]

on his purchases as well as on his sales. The retail price is often more than twice the c.i.f. price, even in towns; in country shops where the majority of the population makes its purchases, the price sometimes exceeds three times the c.i.f. price.

The fact that the middlemen's margins are large does not necessarily mean that they are exorbitant. The enormous distances and the high cost of transport in countries such as Black Africa should not be forgotten. Nevertheless, it follows from the size of these margins that a piece of sharp practice involving only a small proportion of the total price can eat into the real income of the producer to a marked degree. Unfortunately, such acts are still far too common in present-day Africa, especially on the

[1] Senegal.   [2] Ivory Coast.   [3] Chad.
[4] c.i.f. Libreville.
[5] Mekambo trading station.
[6] c.i.f. Pointe-Noire.
[7] 500, shop at Bangui; 700 to 900 up country (Oubangui).
[8] Tennis shoes are the African's normal footwear.
[9] Shop at Bangui.
[10] 2000, shop at Pointe-Noire; up country in West Africa prices for the same product ranging between 2,000 and 3,400 have been noted.

part of small traders who are the first to handle exported goods and the last to handle imported ones. Such abuses take various forms, whether plain overcharging or common forms of deception such as fraud at the weighing machine.

But the peasant is not only a producer and a consumer. He is almost bound to be a borrower as well, because his income is small and comes in irregularly during the year. This necessitates resort to financial middlemen as well as commercial ones.

Ordinary banks, which often provide agricultural credits in developed countries, as well as to Western-type farmers in underdeveloped ones, are involved hardly at all in financing native growers. This gives private, person-to-person credit its great importance. It is very expensive, first because the borrower can offer little in the way of guarantees but chiefly because his need is usually urgent and he is therefore in no position to haggle over terms. Usury is a running sore in underdeveloped countries. Of the states of the French Community, Madagascar is undoubtedly the country where it reaches the most scandalous proportions. But it is met with elsewhere too. It is estimated that out of 73 metropolitan francs which the Senegalese peasant receives on an average for a kilogramme of groundnuts, he pays from 10 to 15 francs as interest on loans contracted during the year in anticipation of his season's takings (of course excluding the repayment of the loans themselves). In the Philippines the rate varies from 25 to 40 per cent per annum. In China Monsieur Dumont has recorded certain cases where 10 per cent was charged for 10 days.[1]

Not only is this private credit very expensive. It has the further disadvantage of accentuating the dependence of the grower upon the landowner or the trader, as the case may be. In the example quoted above by Monsieur Dumont, the intermediary between the landowner and the peasant in a kind of feudal hierarchy borrows from the landowner at 6 per cent for 10 days and relends to the peasant at 10 per cent for 10 days. This greatly increases the peasant's dependence upon the feudal or semi-feudal

[1] *Révolution dans les campagnes chinoises*, p. 34.

powers by which he is ruled. But private credit is far more apt to increase commercial dependence. This is seen very clearly in Black Africa. It is customary to obtain loans from the large trading concerns, or more usually nowadays from the small trader who in turn receives an advance from the large concern, the two successive credits representing an advance on the security of the anticipated harvest. When the harvest is gathered the grower has no choice but to take it to the trader from whom he received his loan. Thus, by losing his freedom to sell to whom he will, he loses a trump card in price negotiations.

Broadly speaking, the small grower in underdeveloped countries exchanges his produce for merchandize, or rather, in most cases, for merchandize and time, since he needs the goods before being able to dispose of his produce. Moreover, the buyer of his produce, the seller of the other goods he needs and the source of financial credit are often one and the same trader. It is easy to see that irrespective of world rates for raw materials, finished goods and credits, there is very little to prevent the middleman from manipulating all three to the disadvantage of the grower.

What can public authorities do to counteract this state of affairs? Control price margins and money-changing operations? The very large areas over which such transactions are current, and the illiteracy of the growers, would nullify such controls. There are only two effective weapons : the development of co-operatives, and direct state intervention in the exchange mechanism with the object either of completely replacing the present system by co-operatives or government agencies, or at least of standardizing prices by the constant threat of competition at normal prices.

Producers' co-operatives have already been developed in many underdeveloped countries, primarily in Asia where in 1950 there were more than 300,000 co-operatives with a total membership of some 50 million people.[1] One of the leading authorities on co-

[1] Twenty-five millions of these were in China, joined up in 45,000 co-operatives (before the communist revolution), 14 millions in India in 120,000 operatives, 4 millions in Pakistan in 50,000 co-operatives, and $3\frac{1}{2}$ millions in Burma in 10,000 co-operatives. The movement has been speeded up in

operation, Monsieur Colombain, says that these co-operatives are often run as well as any in the West. This observation relates particularly to certain parts of India, to East Pakistan and to Malaya.

The idea of co-operation has not penetrated into all fields simultaneously or to the same extent. The only really large-scale attempts to form producers' co-operatives have been made in Communist countries, though examples of agricultural producers' co-operatives can be found in India, Pakistan, Formosa, the Sudan and even in the former Belgian Congo.

Generally speaking, non-Communist countries have kept to the better known forms of co-operative organization. Usually rural credit co-operatives to combat indebtedness and usury have come first; then buyers' co-operatives, and later still sellers' co-operatives. This same chronological sequence appeared in Asia; credit co-operatives were the first to spread and are now of considerable importance[1] particularly in India.[2]

In Black Africa, on the other hand, sellers' co-operatives were started first. In general, co-operation is most strongly developed in Asia, insufficiently so in Africa, and even less in Latin America.

Now co-operation is one of the best possible methods available to mitigate the worst consequences of underdevelopment for native agriculturalists. In the first place it secures to the producers themselves the margins, often excessive, now taken by middlemen; it also seems to offer the most natural channel for propagating improved methods in agriculture and for diffusing expert advice : moreover, it can be made a condition of the grant of co-operative credit that such advice be followed—indeed, price differentials can be used as an incentive and a sanction for the supply of good produce and respect for agricultural advice.

China since the Communist revolution. Dumont (op. cit. p. 77) says that 60 per cent of the Chinese peasants were enrolled in "temporary assistance groups" in 1954. It is claimed that the 100 million families in China had been organized in 1 million kolkhozes by 1960.

[1] There are 130,000 credit co-operatives in Asia.

[2] India has 100,000 credit co-operatives with a total membership of $5\frac{1}{2}$ millions. The movement has existed for a very long time, going back to an important law which was promulgated in 1904.

Most forward-looking managers even in private commerce seem nowadays to be convinced that the development of co-operation is a good thing. During the last few years the large trading concerns in Black Africa have seen fit to close a large proportion of their bush depots, withdrawing as it were to the large centres chiefly because they found that social legislation was affecting the profitability of their operations. The immediate result was an upsurge of smaller traders which, however, often led to the abuses described earlier in this chapter. In consequence, some of the large trading concerns are now prepared to deal directly with the producers' co-operatives, and this in itself will encourage their establishment.

Indispensable though it is, however, the development of the co-operative movement calls for a good deal of prudence, since pitfalls await the unwary which can set back the spread of the idea for years, as has happened in Black Africa. For this reason governments in underdeveloped countries should not only encourage their development by such means as tax concessions, financial assistance or propaganda, but should also keep a close watch over their development. They should also make provision for the training of reliable and competent managers for co-operatives yet to be set up. There may be reason to produce half-way formulas by which opinion among the producers can be led gradually to accept the idea of co-operatives, conditioning them through what might be called "pre-co-operatives."[1]

The most appropriate point for the state to intervene directly in the training cycle is the question of finance.

Public or semi-public organizations can of course play an important part in the commercial sphere, either as half-way houses on the road to co-operation (such are provident societies and rural development mutual societies in the french-speaking countries in Africa) or as controlling bodies in the network of co-

[1] In french-speaking countries in Africa, efforts have been under way for several years to promote the formation of "rural development mutual societies," half way between the old provident societies (officially sponsored producers' mutual societies) and a fully developed co-operative. These intermediate societies give the producer substantially more responsibility than did the old provident societies.

operatives—as well as traditional private business concerns, be it noted, especially as regards the sale of produce abroad. Reference was made in Chapter II[1] to the role of marketing boards and of price stabilization funds, both of which are semi-public organizations.

But state action can go further in relation to the provision of credit. Nearly all underdeveloped countries have found it necessary to set up organizations specializing in the grant of agricultural credits. Sometimes such organizations do not have an independent legal existence but remain simply administrative departments, as in Jordan, Formosa and South Vietnam; but they are most frequently institutions or companies with quasi-banking functions, financed mainly by budgetary credits or perhaps by certain public revenues allocated wholly or partly for the purpose. In some instances the government endeavours to obtain extra capital from other sources; it may for example ask the country's commercial banks to buy shares or otherwise to assist in financing such institutions.

In countries where co-operation is sufficiently developed, the financing authority lends mainly to co-operatives, at low rates of interest, leaving to them the task of advancing credit to their members. This is the situation in many Asian countries, especially in India, Cambodia and the Philippines as well as in Egypt and Spain, and even in some Latin American countries such as Chile. Where, on the other hand, co-operation is not yet widespread, these institutions have to deal directly with the small farmers. Such is the case in Latin America and to a large extent in Black Africa. Experience has shown the method of making loans direct to users to be much less convenient than the other one, as it is far more difficult for a financial institution to hold a correct balance between imprudence on the one hand and over-strict criteria or procedures which defeat the purpose, on the other.

[1] p. 16

Chapter Six

MALTHUS AND THE UNDERPRIVILEGED NATIONS

THE PEASANTS of underdeveloped countries need to be delivered not only from the incubus of landowners and grasping middlemen, but they must also be freed from the burden caused by their own proliferation.

In 1961 there are 3 thousand million people in the world. Every year there are 34 births per thousand human beings, or 102 million at the above population figures, and 18 deaths per thousand, making 54 million. This gives a rate of growth of 16 per thousand, so that in 1961 world population is growing at the rate of 48 million a year, a number equal to the population of a country like France. At this rate the increase in 10 years would exceed 500 million, or roughly as many people as there were in the whole world, in all probability, about the middle of the seventeenth century.

World population will very probably double in 44 years, which means that other things being equal it will reach 6 thousand million early in the twenty-first century.

This demographic explosion is a serious matter if resources—with food in the first place—do not follow the same curve. The

FAO[1] has issued some revealing documents on this subject.[2] It is true that over the greater part of the world (excluding continental China, about which we have insufficient information), food production per head of the population regained its pre-war level in the early fifties, and is now some 14 per cent above it. But it is the most highly developed countries in the world which are mainly responsible for this increase. The Near East is alone among the underdeveloped regions in having witnessed a genuine and sustained rise in production per head above the pre-war level; here it attains approximately 10 per cent. In contrast to this, the Far East (excluding continental China) still averages just about its pre-war level, whilst Africa shows a slight regression of about 1 per cent and Latin America has fallen behind by as much as 5 per cent.

In most of the underdeveloped countries this situation is due to inadequate development of agricultural production combined with an extremely large and rapid population increase. The 1.6 per cent rate of growth of world population shown above is made up of much lower rates for the developed countries (in many cases around 0.5 per cent) and correspondingly higher rates for the underdeveloped countries, generally at least 2 per cent and sometimes approaching or even exceeding 3 per cent as in Ceylon, Puerto Rico, the French Antilles and Reunion.

This situation is due to the success of the fight against sickness and death carried on with the brains and usually with the money of the West. For example, DDT has wiped out malaria in Ceylon and thus lowered the mortality rate from 24.5 per thousand in 1935-9, to 10.4 in 1954. The fight against malaria, tuberculosis, syphilis and epidemic sicknesses such as plague, cholera and typhus has had considerable demographic consequences throughout the indigent countries. Moreover, modern means of transport which enables food to be moved quickly to where it is needed have gradually reduced the incidence of famine. All these causes have combined to bring about a decrease of between 40 and 20 per

[1] Food and Agriculture Organization of the United Nations.
[2] *World Food and Agriculture situation in 1961.* FAO *1961.*

thousand, in round figures, in the space of a few dozen years in the "underprivileged countries" taken as a whole.

But the masses who have been rescued from death have not been saved from extreme poverty. Why? To begin with, it is easier to mobilize goodwill to save life than for raising the standard of living, because the former makes a more insistent appeal to the heart. But more important is the fact that death is easier to combat than is poverty. And the reason for this is undoubtedly the difference in the respective roles of mental and physical activity in the fight against death as compared with those in the fight against poverty. To take medicine as an example: although some forms of treatment may be very expensive, when it comes to dealing with the great social scourges, once the discovery has been achieved it can be made available at relatively small cost. Thus the cost per head of the fight against malaria, which in certain cases has ended in complete victory, varied from a few cents to one dollar according to the country. There is also an intellectual content in economic action—the development of new varieties, for instance, or the study of the possibilities of setting up a new industry, economic planning, and so on; but the cost of the material investment needed to bring these into real existence is much greater. Compared with the dollar that it cost to save a man from malaria, thus considerably increasing his expectation of life, the cost of purchasing modern equipment to create for him new, productive employment averages more than a thousand dollars.

In medicine, the intellectual contribution is predominent; it therefore follows that as soon as the developed countries have made a discovery they can fairly quickly communicate its benefits to the whole world. But in the economic sphere material action is by far the largest ingredient, and consequently it is extremely difficult for underdeveloped countries to imitate the economic strides made by advanced ones.

If, then, the decrease in mortality cannot be balanced by an increase in production, it is natural to think next of decreasing the birthrate. The problem of birth control is of fundamental importance for underdeveloped countries. It appears to have been first practised among the upper classes in France in the eighteenth century, and has since extended progressively to the other classes and to other developed nations; what then are its chances of finding acceptance now among the masses in the underdeveloped countries?

A systematic policy of birth control is certainly feasible, given certain conditions; Japan's example in this respect is striking. In 1948 the Japanese parliament passed a law encouraging contraception and even authorizing, within certain limits, abortion and sterilization. A great propaganda and teaching drive was also launched. In six years the birthrate has fallen by more than one third, i.e. from 33.2 per thousand in 1949, to 19.4 in 1955, and the present rate of growth of the Japanese population is only one per cent per year.

It must however be recognized that a policy of birth control is bound to meet with serious obstacles in an underdeveloped country. There are the obstacles of old customs and lack of understanding; then there are philosophical obstacles : on the whole religions do not favour birth control, one important reason being that they are usually strongly in favour of family life. Nevertheless, several religions show a liberal attitude on the subject. This is true of Islam, Hinduism and the Protestant form of Christianity.

Of the three great philosophical movements which have played an important part in resistance to a world policy of birth restriction, the first is Catholicism which, traditionally, will not allow any method of birth restriction other than continence and, more recently, the Ogino method; secondly there is the movement of Mahatma Ghandi, who for moral reasons allowed only a single method of birth control, namely continence : lastly, there is Communism. It has been stated in several official declarations by the Soviet Union, particularly at the Population Commission of the United Nations, that the problem of over-population was limited to the capitalist world, being a result of private property, and that the idea of restricting births was a "cannibal theory invented by the bourgeois ideologies", as Mr. Kruschev said in 1955.

Hitherto the chief advocates of a policy of birth control over against these hostile movements have been the Americans and the Anglo-Saxons generally, working through various international organizations. The effects of Anglo-Saxon zeal have been felt throughout the non-Communist world, except in countries where it meets with resistance from the Catholics; in spite of the influence of the United States, birth control methods have not spread at all widely up till now in Latin America, with the exception of Porto-Rico. Neither has the birth control movement made much headway in the Mediterranean or in Africa owing to Catholic influence, either direct (as in Spain or Italy) or indirect (as in African countries where Belgian and particularly French authorities were in control).[1]

On the other hand, where there is little or no Catholic influence, the Anglo-Saxon doctrines are vigorously put into effect. This is the position, to speak only of Asia, in Formosa, Hong Kong, Ceylon and Thailand, Malaya, Singapore, Pakistan and Israel. Even in India resistance from Ghandism appears to have been overcome.

In 1957 the policy of Communist China temporarily turned against Moscow orthodoxy on this subject, for a law was passed legalizing abortion and sterilization in certain circumstances, and at the same time a campaign to promote contraception was launched. Furthermore, the legal age for marriage was raised for both men and women. All these measures were officially aimed at reducing the birthrate by 50 per cent in ten years. It seems, however, that this policy met with such resistance and hostility from the Chinese people that it was dropped. Thus the prophecy made in 1952 by Monsieur Alfred Sauvy[2] comes into its own again : "Marx did not foresee the fall in mortality which would cause the average life of a worker in 1950 to be longer than that of a bourgeois in 1850. But as long as Marxism does not hold

---

[1] In France, and hence also in Algeria and in the overseas territories, the law of the 31st July 1920, forbade all propaganda of any sort in favour of birth control.

[2] Alfred Sauvy, *Théorie Générale de la Population*, Vol. I. p. 254.

sway over the whole world it will not openly tackle population problems. The need to bring the birthrate into harmony with the progress of medicine will be rediscovered only later, and then under another name."

It can be said that of the three great sources of resistance to a policy of birth-control, Catholicism today is still the most resolute. The problem is doubtless receiving careful study within the Catholic Church; it is certain that very many Catholic laymen, including convinced believers, no longer see this crucial problem in terms entirely of black and white. For example, in France the situation in Africa, and particularly in Algeria, inevitably highlights the problem, and it is widely felt to be a paradox that the influence of traditional Catholic opinion in Paris resulted for so long in the isolation of Algeria, which is a Muslim country, from the great movement for population control which exists in most underdeveloped countries.

Over the last 15 years inventions have followed so fast upon one another that the possibility of Mathus's being proved wrong a few years hence cannot be excluded; it may be that the earth, made fruitful by human intelligence, will prove capable of feeding from 10 to 20 thousand million human beings. But this is only a supposition, and humanity can hardly be invited to play poker for such high stakes. Birth control takes some time to become socially effective, and there is little time to be lost if a catastrophe in the indigent and overpopulated countries is to be avoided.

Granted, then, that a systematic policy of birth limitation is indispensable, by what means is it to be put into operation?

Birth control is expensive. The only widely used methods which are both safe and cheap call for self-denial by the individual, who has to renounce pleasure or consent to a diminution of it. Recent research in the United States has produced a pill which will induce temporary sterility, a method that is simple and, above all, cheap. Clearly, this discovery is a considerable event in human history. But until it becomes generally available, even methods as imperfect as the Ogino system can be useful in underdeveloped countries. Though an individual couple cannot rely with complete certainty on their effect, they are of greater value on the national scale, for statistical reasons. It may be observed here that for certain primitive mentalities the presentation of the Ogino method may take on the glamour of an apparently magical formula.

However this may be, it costs a lot even to teach a method. Hundreds of millions of men and women have to be made to understand and induced to accept things which are not easily comprehensible, acceptable or applicable. This is costly; there is a case for large-scale financial assistance from the rich nations and from international organizations for this piece of technical assistance—for such it is.

At the same time everything possible should be done to minimise the risk that a teaching campaign financed from outside the country might be looked upon as Western egoism in a new form. Some observers in Japan are uneasy, because planned parenthood suffers from the original sin of having been introduced from America. Might not a surge of anti-Western feeling accompanying a resurgence of nationalism be in danger of upsetting the policy of birth limitation, thus bringing about a new urge towards ethnic expansion? In Africa, birth control should in no circumstances be allowed to look like a modern facet of colonialism. People must not be led to say : "When the colonies were exploited and liable to forced labour at pleasure, you were not afraid of an increase in population because it gave you more cheap labour. But nowadays the relations between developed and underdeveloped countries have been reversed, and the duties and costs equal or even outweigh the advantages. Africans are becoming expensive; therefore you want to restrict their production." *For this reason, it is essential that the real leaders of the indigent nations should be convinced of the usefulness of birth control and should themselves advocate it.* In this sphere, as in so many others, policies can be carried through only by the real leaders.[1] But even if these financial and political conditions are

[1] cf. Chapter XIII.

fulfilled, complete success cannot be expected unless the birth control policy is linked to a policy of all-round development. Some writers maintain that a policy of birth control simply will not work in an underdeveloped country because the birthrate there is closely bound up with other factors. Thus Madame Germaine Tillion[1] has written : "It is just as absurd to preach birth control to a primitive population as it would be to recommend its abolition among university circles in Paris, or New York." We shall soon known whether this pessimism is fully justified, because there are some important experiments under way. But there quite certainly is a connection which is difficult to break, between underdevelopment and an uncontrolled birthrate. After all, any action resulting from the will to organize the future—and birth control is such an act—connotes a certain ability to forgo present satisfaction; such abstinence is not possible in extreme poverty. Moreover, one of the basic reasons for birth restriction in the West has been the qualitative idea of posterity. A Western couple, even in modest circumstances, consider that their child has the right to good food, a good education, good holidays, a good job and often a small endowment; his parents realize that, even with help from the state, they cannot give such a standard of life to a large number of children. But when the child has no rights except the right to live, and to the modest sustenance which our Heavenly Father is said to give to the very birds, this deep inhibition no longer exists. For birth control to become effective this brake must obviously come into play, which implies a change in the whole conception of society such as occurs when the underdeveloped country becomes economically and socially a modern country, or at least one which is firmly on the road to modernization.

Birth restriction and economic development must therefore go hand in hand. It would be vain to hope to adjust the population of poor countries to the present level of their production by a policy of birth limitation sufficient to balance the decrease in mortality. To be successful, birth control must be allied with other

[1] *L'Algerie en 1957*, p. 37.

dynamic policies within the nation and form one aspect of them.

The West has lowered the death-rate within the under-privileged nations. It thus has a clear duty to help them either to decrease the birth-rate by a similar amount or to carry through their economic metamorphosis. What I have said, however, shows that these are not alternatives, but two aspects of the same thing.

Part II

WAYS OF GROWTH

Chapter Seven

CONDITIONS OF GROWTH

THE SIX preceding chapters dealt with the problems of distribution or sharing. Assuming the production of an underdeveloped country to be at a given level, we have examined the steps to be taken to secure for the country, or within the country for the primary producer, the largest possible income. In Part Two of this book, which begins with the present chapter, we no longer take the production of a country as being fixed; we shall be studying the conditions for its growth.

In the real world these two types of question are of course closely bound up with one another, so much so that we have already had much to say about development. For most of the measures mentioned in connection with problems of distribution are also relevant to the question of growth. For example, an improvement in the terms of trade would add to the amounts available for local investment. The best way to encourage a grower to increase his production is to give him a good price for his products and make it as stable as possible. If it is a question of attracting capital from outside, one of the basic methods is bound up with local taxation. And finally, family limitation is undertaken with a view to improving the nation's posterity, and this can be a crucial element in growth.

We now have to examine the problems of development in

themselves, that is to say, the policy of investment in under-developed countries. What are the sources of capital? What are the most suitable ways of putting it to work? We shall endeavour to throw some light on the first of these questions in Chapters VII to X and on the second in Chapters XI to XIII.

In dealing with the financial problems of growth it is necessary first to make an estimate of the volume of investment needed to attain a given target of development.[1]

If the objective is to raise the income of a country to a certain level by the end of a given period, what amount of capital should be regarded as necessary in relation to the increase of income thus defined? The relation between increase of income and capital is called by economists the co-efficient of capital-intensity. If, in order to raise the annual income of a country by 100 an investment of 400 is needed, the co-efficient of capital-intensity is said to equal 4 (this is the Anglo-Saxon presentation and the most commonly used; the equation can also be reversed, in which case we say that the "national rate of interest" is 25 per cent).

Naturally the co-efficient varies according to the operation we have in mind. Indeed, theoretically it could vary from zero to infinity. Take as the two extremes, on the one hand a prodigious operation in which owing to incredible assistance from nature a huge basin could be irrigated with just a few strokes of the pick, and on the other hand an expensive and utterly foolish investment which would prove to be useless when completed.

Thus when calculating co-efficient of capital-intensity each case must be taken on its merits; it should form one of the basic criteria in evaluating any investment proposal. Nor is it an easy task. It would be comparatively easy if it were just a matter of comparing the cost of the investment with the amount of income to which it immediately gives rise within the country where the investment is made, by the working of the factory, the dam or the plantation envisaged. But when these primary incomes are spent they will create secondary incomes, and these in their turn

[1] The most thorough study of this subject is: Leon Tabah, *Le Problème Population-Investissement-Niveau de vie dans les pays sous-développés*, pp. 227-8 of the symposium entitled *Le Tiers Monde*.

will lead to tertiary incomes and so on. These successive waves become smaller and smaller, since at each stage part of the money is used to buy products which are imported into the country, and only the remainder goes to increase the income of the country itself; assuming that a constant fraction is spent on imports, we arrive at a decreasing geometrical progression.[1] Estimating the effect on the national income of a certain proposed investment, or even of one which has been carried out, is therefore a delicate task calling for detailed knowledge of the structure and mechanism of the national economy. The most that can be said is that the calculation is bound to be easier for an underdeveloped country than for a developed one because there are fewer branches of the economy to set in motion.

But though it is indispensable to calculate the co-efficient of capital-intensity in order to evaluate a given product, we are here concerned not with the co-efficient which might be called analytical (operation by operation) but with the synthesis of these co-efficients, that is to say one which measures this same relationship between capital and income for an aggregate of operations effected in a given country during a given period.

Strictly speaking, the only way to determine this synthesized co-efficients with complete accuracy is to use the analytical method first, which means working out a coherent plan composed of a number of related operations and estimating by concrete analysis of the actions and reactions of these various operations the increase of income to which it would give rise. Or rather, the best procedure would be to agree upon a certain hypothetical increase of income desired over a determined period in a given country and then to make a study of the ways and means of doing this, at the conclusion of which the various investment expenses needed for the objects in view could be added together. In other words, if the calculation of the synthesized co-efficient is done with complete thoroughness, it is almost indistinguishable from the act of planning itself. Any other method must of necessity yield only a very rough approximation.

[1] cf. Chapter III, p. 39.

Nevertheless, even when overall planning for an under-developed country is still in the initial stage it is useful to have some knowledge of the scale on which the capital is needed to attain a certain rate of development in the country in question. Is there an average co-efficient of capital-intensity which would give a rough and ready approximation? Mr. Colin Clark was the first to do such calculations for the year 1913;[1] according to him the co-efficient varies from 3.5 for Austria to 5.85 for Argentina; the principal developed countries of the period have a co-efficient either between 4 and 5, or very close to this bracket. Later, the same author[2] assembled some data by means of which the co-efficient could be calculated for more recent years and, more interestingly, for several years in succession, for various countries which are now industrialized. His conclusion is that a co-efficient of 4 is the average figure giving the least inaccurate idea of the reality.

But most of these calculations, whether by Mr. Colin Clark or those who have followed him, relate to developed countries because there is too little information about the others. We want to know whether the co-efficient for underdeveloped countries is higher or lower than that for industrialized ones. The experts differ on this point; arguments can be advanced on both sides. In support of a higher co-efficient it can be said that non-productive investments will be numerous and heavy in a country which does not possess the basic economic equipment. On the other hand, it can be maintained that agricultural techniques are often so rudimentary in underdeveloped countries that only a relatively small expense is needed to bring a much greater return for the labour done; furthermore, in overpopulated countries agriculture is overloaded with people who on balance produce nothing, or even less than nothing, and if they are moved to other productive work the national income is bound to increase noticeably.

It must be admitted that our knowledge is too much in its

---

[1] *The Conditions of Economic Progress*, pp. 374-422 especially p. 389.
[2] The economy of underdeveloped countries, *Review of Economic Progress*, April-June 1952, pp. 1-12.

infancy to give a really convincing answer to this question. M. Kuznets[1] thinks that the co-efficient rises at the beginning of the growth period, then remains stationary for a middle period and finally drops once more when the country has attained a high level of development. But we are not justified in drawing any conclusions from this as regards underdeveloped countries. In actual fact there is general agreement to take as a basis a figure somewhere near the co-efficient of 4, advanced by Mr. Colin Clark. Singer[2] has worked out a model for a typical under-developed economy in which he assumes a co-efficient of 4 for agriculture and 6 for non-agricultural operations, thus making an average of 5. Mr. Arthur Lewis[3] uses a co-efficient varying between 3 and 4 for underdeveloped countries. M. Rosenstein-Rodan[4] uses the co-efficient of 4. Data assembled by the French Ministry for Overseas Territories[5] has given a co-efficient, which is remarkably constant from one year to another, of 4.2 per cent over the last twelve years for all French territories in Africa ex-cepting the states of Arab population.[6] Subject to the reservation indicated above, we can work on an average co-efficient of some-where between 4 and 5 for underdeveloped countries generally.

[1] Population, Income and Capital (*International Bulletin of the Social Sciences*, UNESCO 1954, No. II, p. 186).
[2] The Mechanics of Economic Development. A Quantitative Model Approach, *The Indian Economic Review*, August 1952, pp. 2-18.
[3] *The Theory of Economic Growth*, pp. 201-207.
[4] Capital Needs in Underdeveloped Countries. *Economie* Appliquée, June 1954.
[5] Statistics for which M. Maldant was responsible.
[6] For the understanding of these figures it should be made clear, firstly that we are speaking of the relation between additional national product and additional capital. The much more nebulous problem of the relation between total national product and total national capital is disregarded. Secondly, social investments are included when calculating capital (Mr. Colin Clark shows this quite clearly and the calculations of the French Ministry for Overseas Territories are based on the same principle). For it would be arbitrary to distinguish in this field between economic investments and social investments, since national growth necessarily implies that the various components develop in roughly the same way. Thirdly, the calculations of the French Foreign Ministry are based on the one hand on gross national pro-duct and on the other hand on gross additions to capital; in any case, as we are dealing with underdeveloped countries, it makes little difference to the result which basis we choose i.e. gross national product as against national income, or gross or net additions to capital. In either case we are dealing with roughly the same order of size.

The total of the national products of these countries can be put at slightly more than one hundred thousand million dollars.[1] It follows that an increase of one per cent, at the present level of national product in the indigent countries taken as a whole, would require between 4 and 5 thousand million dollars of investment.

We shall now try to determine the minimum rate of development which can be regarded as reasonable. It was noted in an earlier chapter that the populations of underdeveloped countries usually increase by between 2 and 3 per cent per year, and the average is probably between 2 and 2.5 per cent—probably nearer 2 per cent. Thus, simply to maintain the *per capita* income in underdeveloped countries, annual investments approaching 10 per cent (2—2.5 multiplied by 4 or 5) of the national product of the countries in question are required. But to raise the *per capita* income additional investment would be required. Suppose an annual rate of increase of *per capita* incomes of between 4 and 5 per cent is aimed at; this would call for the investment of further sums of the order of 20 per cent of the national product (4 or 5 multiplied by 4 or 5).

In total, then, the maintenance of this rate of growth would require the annual investment of 30 per cent of the national product of the underdeveloped countries, which amounts to slightly more than thirty thousand million dollars at the present level, and this figure would increase from year to year at the same rate as the national product itself : that is to say, by approximately 6 to $7\frac{1}{2}$ per cent per annum.

In the preceding argument we have not distinguished between gross investment and net investment. There is a considerable difference between the two in developed countries, because the amortization of existing investments alone absorbs substantial

---

[1] This figure is only an overall approximation; it assumes for each one of the one thousand eight hundred and fifty million human beings in underdeveloped countries an income per head of approximately 55 dollars per year. Many underdeveloped countries, particularly in Latin America and in Africa, have *per capita* incomes considerably higher, but there can be no doubt that the two great underdeveloped areas of the world, India and China, are slightly below this figure.

savings. In underdeveloped countries, on the other hand, it is permissible to forgo this distinction when making a first approximation owing to the small value of the already existing investments.

We therefore reach the conclusion that it should be possible by investing, at the present stage, about 30 thousand million dollars each year to ensure an increase in *per capita* incomes of the order of 4 to 5 per cent in the underdeveloped countries. This would no doubt be a very welcome achievement in the poorer country, but it should be borne in mind that progress at this rate would not reduce or even hold at its present level the difference in absolute value which exists between the *per capita* income in rich countries and that in poorer countries. For if we assume, as is reasonable, that *per capita* income in the rich countries increases by 3 per cent each year, then by raising that of the poorer countries by 4 or 5 per cent we are indeed giving them a relatively higher rate of growth, but one which is lower in absolute value. 4 or 5 per cent of the income of an inhabitant of Black Africa is very much less than 3 per cent of the income of somebody living in metropolitan France.

Evidently, the estimated requirement at which we have arrived in this chapter by no means constitutes an ideal programme; all we can say is that figures put forward give some idea of a reasonable minimum.

But how is this thirty thousand million dollars to be obtained?

Chapter Eight

SAVINGS IN POOR COUNTRIES

THERE IS precious little hope of seeing the underdeveloped countries make this thirty thousand million dollars available from their own national product.

Most authors consider that the majority of underdeveloped countries save about 5 per cent of their national income (Lewis says 4 to 5 per cent,[1] Bettelheim says 5 to 7 per cent,[2]). A study made by the National Institute of Statistics in France,[3] which arranges the countries of the world into 4 groups according to whether their net investment represents over 15 per cent, between 10 and 15 per cent, between 5 and 10 per cent, or less than 5 per cent of national income, shows that for the period 1948 to 1949 most of the developed countries were in the first or second group whilst the underdeveloped countries were found in the fourth group (India, China, Afghanistan, Iran, Iraq, Syria, Lebanon, Spain and Portugal), or in the third (several Latin American countries, Egypt, Bulgaria and Rumania), seldom in the second (Brazil, Mexico and Peru). Only two (Yugoslavia and Southern Rhodesia) were found in the top group.[4]

[1] *The Theory of Economic Growth,* p. 207 et seq., and 225 et seq.

[2] Sous développement et Planification, *Politique Étrangère,* No. III, 1957, p. 293.

[3] *Quelques aspects fondamentaux de l'économie mondiale,* INSEE, 1951, p. 173 et seq.

[4] It should however be noted that the list of countries examined is not complete, since no data were available for certain countries.

These statements should be treated with some reserve. It is not certain that the figures on which the calculations are based are very reliable. In many instances sufficient weight is not given to investments in kind, such as the clearance of land for cultivation, and irrigation works done by the people concerned themselves, or the planting of perennial crops or the building of rural housing. One study of the African countries in the French Community showed a rate of savings equal to nearly 20 per cent of the gross national product. These countries probably have a relatively high rate for underdeveloped countries, and we shall try to show in the next chapter why this is so?[1] Nevertheless an assumed rate of investment as low as 5 per cent for underdeveloped countries taken as a whole does not seem to be very well founded.

However this may be, the savings are not nearly adequate for the needs of development. The reasons for this relative lack of national savings in underdeveloped countries are not hard to find. The principal cause is the smallness of the national income itself. An analysis of marginal factors makes it clear, as common sense also tells us, that ability to save increases disproportionately to the growth of individual income.

The countries in question are of course often characterized by great inequalities of wealth. There are rich people in poor countries, and some very rich ones. But it is precisely the way these rich people behave which is the second cause of low overall savings. They spend on luxuries, whether locally, or abroad in modern countries where living is good. Even when they save they seldom make productive use of their savings, tending rather to spend them on palaces or jewels, or even to hoard them (hoarding is estimated to account for 10 per cent of the national income in many underdeveloped countries).

Besides rich people of feudal or near-feudal type, rich people of the colonial or near-colonial type use their savings in a more modern manner, but its effect within the country is no different

[1] pp. 91-2.

since the money is very often invested outside the underdeveloped country itself.

A third cause should also be included in the analysis. When there is an increase in the income of the mass of the people, or part of the mass, by reason either of some initial investment or of an improvement in the terms of trade, or of a reduction in feudal or near-feudal burdens, there is a strong temptation to use this surplus income for consumption instead of saving. Such a temptation is understandable in countries where the standard of life is low or wretched, and two things conspire to strengthen it still further. On the one hand the man who has got more money sees his increased income dissipated in maintaining a larger fraction of his family (in the wider sense of the word), which flocks around him on hearing the news. The origin of this custom is the very strong sense of kinship and tradition of hospitality which has existed in the underdeveloped countries since ancient times.[1] On the other hand, the sight of the standard of living of developed countries increases the wish to consume; the sight of others who are better off is constantly before their eyes because they travel either in person or vicariously with the aid of the press, photography, the radio and the cinema; in addition, developed countries often have their extensions into underdeveloped countries

[1] Observing what happens in this respect in the United States, France and Black Africa, one is tempted to say that family feeling in the limited meaning of the words (wife and children) has a dynamogenic effect and is one of the basic factors in economic progress, in that it encourages the effort to increase income or capital for the sake of the home; whereas family feeling in the larger meaning of the term (parents, grandparents and more or less distant relatives of the same generation) puts a brake on economic progress, because the younger generation is immobilised by its family (as happens in France) since the latter exerts a strong attraction to remaining in the vicinity and thus gives the economic and social unit much less mobility than might be desirable. Worse still, it may rob the member of the tribe who has succeeded a little better than the others, thus taking from him the desire to be more successful.

One sees young Africans coming back to their homeland having obtained a diploma in Paris and thereby a good job, but almost ashamed of their good fortune; as if to excuse themselves they send little presents to their more or less distant relatives; the word soon gets round and nephews and cousins are quick to profit from the good fortune which has come to the family. This happens with such seeming inevitability that if an African wishes to escape from it he has to insist upon being posted to a district other than his own native locality.

in the form of mines, modern industry, or government administrations in colonial territories, and all these display the mode of living that richer countries are able to offer.

Difficult though it is to bring about local saving, it is nonetheless very necessary. It is improbable that aid from abroad can be given in sufficient quantity to meet all the needs adumbrated in Chapter VII; Chapters IX and X will show that external aid only amounts to one sixth of the indispensable minimum. It is certainly desirable that the contribution of the rich nations should be increased, but it is also wise for the poor nations to rely first of all on themselves.

In any event, even if it were possible it would not be desirable for all investment requirements to be met by external aid, for this matter also has qualitative aspects. Man is so made that he does not really benefit from something which costs him nothing.

Development connot be implanted from outside; it must be consciously willed by the developing country, and this will should be made evident by its own efforts, in effort, sacrifices and a general increase of tension within the nation itself. Countries which are helped artificially by rich nations always behave like spoilt children; they are wasteful, superficial and ill-mannered.

What then are the means by which local savings can be made to grow? Monetary investments should be considered first, then investment in kind.

To develop the former, a measure of compulsion should go hand in hand with exhortation.

The best known means of compulsion is, of course, the use of the budget and taxation. Indispensable though this is at all times, it can yield sure results when prices of raw materials are high. In such periods no weakness should be shown by the government. Besides taxation there is, of course, the forced loan, which is particularly useful in reconciling the legitimate salary demands of skilled key workers with what a poor country can afford, by means of the "pécule" system, whereby a part of the salary is compulsorily invested in nationally approved schemes. There is also what might be called compulsory shareholding. To finance the building of a steelworks at Paz del Rio, the Government of Colombia compelled taxpayers to pay supplementary taxes in exchange for which they were given shares in the undertaking.

To encourage voluntary savings by the public, a government should first see that the procedure is made as simple and convenient as possible with a number of different channels through which savings can be made. These include credit establishments, savings banks and travelling banks which have been thoughtfully provided in certain cases, to make more direct contact with a dispersed population. There must also be savings propaganda, or rather the public must be educated as to the necessity for savings. It is a great help towards this understanding if the public can be made to see their interest in investing by providing for a certain connection between savings gathered in a given region, or even a group of villages, and the public works which are undertaken there. This creates a very healthy association of ideas. But it is vital for the authorities to avoid the damaging publicity which would be caused by the loss of savings. It is more important in an underdeveloped country than in a developed one to pay a strict regard to the safety of savings, precisely because the habit of saving has not taken such strong root there.

Another essential point is to encourage those forms of investment which go hand in hand with the spirit of enterprise; the entrepreneur in Schumpeter's sense of the word should be encouraged. To this end Lewis suggests that those who live from unearned income, particularly ground rents, should be mulcted and the proceeds given to those who live from profits[1] unless the former agree to change into the latter—a sociological mutation which, difficult and unlikely though it is, nevertheless has a precedent: that of the Japanese landed gentry who round about 1880 were able to transform themselves into a capitalist class.

But Mr. Lewis is quite as hard on the poor as he is on the rich. At no time does he mention any redistribution of wealth. Both

[1] op. cit. pp. 233-9.

Lewis[1] and Sauvy[2] rightly believe not in levelling but in making the peaks less high; not in using the mountains to fill in the valleys of the social landscape, but in using the mountain tops as far as possible for investment. In the short run this is a harsh solution for the valleys, but it gives them greater future opportunities.

Such is the stern law of growth. Whether in Great Britain, Japan or the USSR, development had been achieved by allocating the fruits of increasing production not to the consuming classes—the workers and peasants—but to investment, either via private enterprise or through state undertakings; and it is not of first importance whether it went to one or the other. However, if the poorer classes are to accept this situation, they must not be consumed by a sense of injustice; and this is one more reason for lopping the incomes of the rich by inducing them to invest a large part of their profits.

But there are two aspects to inequality—the internal inequalities within an underdeveloped country, and those which strike the inhabitant of a poor country when he sees the citizens of a rich one. We have already seen that this juxtaposition is inimical to development. European countries have passed through two phases since the XVIth century. First of all the number of non-agricultural jobs increased without attracting a noticeably higher real wage than the agricultural one; then, when industry had exhausted the pool of potential peasant recruits[3] the number of non-agricultural jobs increased more slowly whilst the remuneration of the urban individual also increased.[4] Owing to the contagious examples of European wages,[5] countries such as those of

[1] ibid., p. 235.

[2] *Théorie Générale de la Population,* Vol. I, pp. 248-251.

[3] This of course means relative, not absolute, exhaustion, having regard to the structure and method of agriculture of the period and in the country in question. In a country with a very custom-bound agricultural structure, such as France, the threshold was reached quite quickly.

[4] cf. Lewis, op. cit., p. 238.

[5] This is how the example catches on : the European wage earner in Africa wishes to have real wages equal to those of a wage earner in Europe, plus a large expatriation bonus. The African wage earner demands equal pay with Europeans for equal work, (a demand which, as far as administrative workers are concerned, has been officially granted in countries which were then French territories by the Law of June 30th 1950 known as the Lamine Gueye Law, which lays it down that management officials are to be paid according to the designation of their job, irrespective of racial origin).

Black Africa are behaving as if they wanted to perform the feat of telescoping these two phases into a single one. But both history and reflection show clearly that the chances of rapid development are bound up with the maintenance of urban incomes at a level close to that of rural ones, and that the public and private savings thus freed constitute the sinews of growth.

This is the real explanation of what Winston Churchill christened the Iron Curtain. Its purpose is to prevent the fascination of the West's way of life from dazzling the inhabitants of countries in which the authorities wish to maintain a low standard of consumption to facilitate rapid development. Just as Ulysses had himself lashed to the mast so that he might not heed the seductive voices of the sirens, so does a steady journey of the nation towards prosperity demand the resoluteness to shun present enjoyments. Nor were the Russians the inventors of iron curtains. At the end of the nineteenth century the Japanese set one up to conceal their own development. The British had no need of one, since they were the first; sailing over a sea devoid of sirens, they could call for greater efforts from all the crew without any fear of defections.

It is no accident that the curtain is known as an iron one, for it is there to safeguard a country's development, and this means primarily its industrialization. Without an iron curtain there will be no steel, for steel is likely then to take second place to butter —in the words of a well-remembered formula which is true also of non-warlike preparations.

There is not the same need for iron curtains everywhere and at all times. Other things being equal, its utility to a country wishing to develop its resources increases with the passage of time, because as methods of disseminating information become more efficient the voice of the sirens is heard ever more strongly. An iron curtain is specially important also to a country which, either from choice or necessity, undertakes development without outside help. Help from outside does indeed mitigate the rigours of this isolation, but a certain degree of separation is nevertheless always essential. Especially in poor countries having close links with rich ones, anything like a correlation of living standards must be avoided or, if the damage has already occurred, gradually eliminated.

But monetary investment is not enough: underdeveloped countries must also make use of investment in kind. Since all that most of the inhabitants of underdeveloped countries possess are their arms, it is their arms that must provide what is saved. Normally the worker is rewarded in cash, and part of this money is set aside for investment. But when monetary incomes are very limited, the attempt can be made to canalize working effort directly into investment projects, like steam condensing straight into ice without passing through the liquid phase.

This can often be done in underdeveloped countries which suffer chronic "concealed unemployment,"[1] as in overpopulated countries, people are crowded into agriculture for want of any other work to do. The marginal product is zero or even a negative quantity, since the men get in one another's way and end up by producing less than would a smaller number from the same amount of land. This situation is found in South-East Asia, the Middle East and certain parts of the Caribbean (Puerto Rico). Some observers consider that "concealed unemployment" affects between 40 per cent and 50 per cent of the rural population in Egypt. If we imagine a piece of land from which x men could obtain the maximum return with the present techniques currently in use in the country, and if in addition to x men there are also y men working on this land, who do nothing to help, and may even hinder, the x group; then it follows that although the x group, by producing more than it consumes, gives rise to "virtual savings", these savings are lost because they go to feed group y. These virtual savings would become real savings if group x continued to feed group y and group y were used on non-agricultural tasks such as public works.

Virtual savings, then, can be actualized in overpopulated countries, with which Nurkse's book deals. One may add that a

[1] On concealed unemployment see NURKSE, *Problems of capital formation in underdeveloped countries,* pp. 32 et seq.

similar technique can often be applied even in countries without excess population, for two reasons. First, relatively slight technical improvements may bring about a sharp increase in the productivity of agricultural labour, thus freeing part of the force without a check to total production. Again, many commodities do not require labour all the year round. In Senegal, for example, rural workers employed in groundnut cultivation are at work for only three or four months of the year.[1] It is thus fair to say that there is in most underdeveloped countries a potential untapped source of labour that could be used to create capital goods for the benefit of the nation. How is this labour to be mobilized? The answer is : by a duality of means similar to that indicated for monetary investments—compulsory savings together with propaganda for voluntary savings.

In the above context, compulsory savings take the form of civic service through work on projects of national interest. It is surely not unreasonable to suggest that young Africans living in the French Community, and not subject to military service, could give their respective countries some months of their time to carrying out such tasks. In this respect, three periods can be distinguished in the history of the French territories. In the colonial period, forced work could be carried out under conditions perhaps not always approved by the local population. Some sixteen years ago a second phase was entered, in which authority was still in the hands of foreigners but was counterbalanced, and sometimes cancelled out, by local political forces acting critically and negatively. During this phase, nothing could be done which had the appearance of forced labour. But now we are in the third phase : power is in indigenous hands, and what a foreign administration was unable to impose, national rulers can induce their people to accept and carry through in the name of a national movement and a common will to advance.

Voluntary savings are achieved by giving to various limited groups some advantages, such as the grant of credits for equip-

---

[1] Discontinuously from the end of July until November.

ment, on condition that the group itself contributes an agreed amount of savings in kind. The lesson of Southern Italy is instructive here. Those who were to benefit from a certain land improvement scheme were first selected; then they all worked together for a year on the basic installations, after which each one received his own parcel of land, and the unity of the group of peasants who had worked together was preserved by various co-operative installations and pieces of equipment held in common.

But great strides have been made during the last twenty-five years in the theory and practice of a new technique, that of financing without previous savings. Can this be done in underdeveloped countries too, even though Keynes had mainly developed countries in mind? Monsieur Jean Ehrhard replied :[1] "Underdeveloped economies are not Keynesian."—a very disputable statement.

Speaking about Black Africa, Ehrhard says[2] : "Agricultural production is inelastic in relation to demand in the short term; that is to say, it does not respond to an increase in income." But an examination of the economic development of African countries in the French Community shows the opposite to be true. Even without private investments, the production of foodstuffs has developed along with total production during the last ten years.[3]

The fact is that in countries of this type there is real underemployment of men and lands, and production is often held back by insufficient demand. Naturally, bottlenecks occur in production from time to time; but these can in many instances be overcome by a relatively small effort. It does therefore seem that increased demand (which can be brought about by a policy of

[1] *Le destin du colonialisme,* p. 212.
[2] ibid., p. 213.
[3] This development of foodstuff production when the income of an African country increases is brought about through a rise in the price of foodstuffs which causes food producers to try to produce them in greater quantity. This is an additional effort, which does not replace an existing one. Thus the Keynesian effect is as complete as possible.

monetary injection) is able effectively to influence the level of production.

This analysis is much less true of overpopulated countries which suffer from under-employment of labour but not of land. In such countries land cannot correctly be said to form a bottleneck. Though not underemployed it may still be badly employed, so much so that a comparatively small effort can produce a good deal more from it to meet solvent demand. It nonetheless remains true that the economies of overpopulated countries are, in Ehrhard's terminology, hardly Keynesian. But they have the compensating advantage that, as we saw above, there is more scope in them for mobilizing virtual savings.

A refusal to adopt Keynesian types of solution for underdeveloped countries may indeed be justified by pointing to the dangers which attend their ill-considered adoption. Inflation, which is always an evil, has in addition some special ill-effects in underdeveloped countries; in fact, it can completely upset the process of growth. So Keynesianism should on no account be used as an ideological camouflage for a weak and opportunist course. The issue of money, either through a budget deficit or expansion of bank credit, may facilitate development; but this does not mean that uncontrolled inflation will do so, still less the reckless prodigality of administrative budgets leading to waste and premature expansion of consumption. Keynesianism must not be used as an excuse for irregularities of this sort.

It is nonetheless true that a monetary injection can be an effective if dangerous weapon in underdeveloped countries, and particularly in those that are not overpopulated. Moreover, the danger can be lessened if the country in question forms part of a monetary area larger than itself, not only because any inflationary tendencies will to some extent become diluted throughout the entire area,[1] but also because it is very much more likely that in a large and complex area an increase in production will furnish

[1] These remarks are true only of a monetary area in which the currencies of its constituent members can be exchanged against one another without restriction and at a fixed rate, and where goods and capital can circulate quite freely.

the goods required by the demand incited by the injection of money.

Let us assume Madagascar to be a monetary area on its own. Then the effect of a monetary injection will be to increase the demand for various commodities, some of which can be grown or manufactured in the country over and above the previous production, whilst others cannot. As regards the former, the effect is favourable, since there is an increase in economic activity; but as regards the latter it is unfavourable, since there is a danger that inflation will be set up. Now let us assume that the first category includes foodstuffs; the second category will certainly include many manufactured products. Madagascar can of course order them from abroad, but in so far as she is not in a position to export additional goods of like value, either foreign countries will not sell her the goods or the terms of trade will deteriorate— prices will rise or, which comes to the same thing, the exchange rate will be lowered.

As Madagascar forms part of the franc area, the first category includes all commodities which the area can produce over and above their previous level. If the injection takes place at a time when certain branches of metropolitan industry are running at less than capacity, these branches will feel the stimulus. The second, or inflation-producing category, will be smaller, and in addition the inflationary tendency will be diluted over the whole area.

This of course does not mean that an underdeveloped country which belongs to a larger area can afford a monetary injection of any size at any time. On the contrary, as we have seen, the right moment depends largely upon the economic structure of the area on the one hand, and on the prevailing economic circumstances on the other hand. The main thing is to ensure that most of the demand will effect goods the production of which can be increased. Thus the operation should be completely controlled, and not by Madagascar alone but by the whole of the franc area, which would bear the brunt of any inflation that was produced. In other words, France can reasonably admit Madagascar into the franc area only if France herself has some voice in Madagascar's monetary policy, which should be worked out by the two countries together.[1]

---

[1] At present, appearances notwithstanding, there is in the countries of the French Community a policy of monetary injection. This is not carried out by the normal issuing institutions. We shall see in Chapter XV that an important part of France's financial aid to the African member countries of the French Community can be likened to a monetary injection. (p. 176. Note 2.)

Chapter Nine

"THE LORD WILL PROVIDE"

I T I S no new idea for a nation to receive help from abroad for its development. The rapid growth of the United States was made possible by timely supplies of men and money from Europe. Even countries which have grown behind an iron curtain have owed much to foreign aid; this is true both of Japan and Russia. As regards the latter, important though the drive of the Soviet Government over the last thirty years has been, take-off goes back to the years before the first world war, during which Western countries allowed her liberal supplies of capital.

It is the nations of Western Europe, and especially Great Britain, who received the smallest amount of what can properly be described as foreign aid towards their development—though it should be added without, we hope, too much play upon words, that by exploiting the rest of the world thanks to the start they had over it, they received from other nations a kind of involuntary aid.

The question of foreign aid is fundamental to the study of the development prospects of today's backward countries. The present chapter deals with aid from public sources and the next one with aid from private sources.

Although most indigent countries loudly demand aid from

public sources, it is subject to two convergent attacks, which could be said to come from the right and left respectively.

The attack from the right found widespread expression in America just after the second world war. Little reliance was placed upon public aid and much on private foreign investment, a panacea the supposed virtues of which have turned to disappointments year after year. Yet this idea gained a new lease of life during the Republican régime.

The attack from the left consists in saying that a nation should finance its own development. Thus Monsieur Bettelheim[1] actually maintained that underdeveloped nations should receive technical rather than financial assistance from the developed nations.

A discussion of these two points of view will bring out more clearly the advantages of public aid. On the one hand private investment, desirable though on the whole it is, can only partially solve the problems of financing. For one thing, it is not concerned with social expenditures. Then again, it presupposes the existence of the basic economic substructure, though in certain circumstances it can carry the cost of this, as happens in some large projects in Africa.[2] Such enterprises however, in the nature of things, present exceptionally favourable circumstances for this devolution of responsibilities, which in general are best left to the public authorities. Furthermore, even for setting up mining, industrial or even agricultural undertakings, private capitalists frequently seek the participation of public finance in the form of shares or, most often, of loans.

Much can be expected of private investment, but a certain minimum of public investment is needed to give it optimum

---

[1] In an article entitled: "Sous-développment et planification", *Politique étrangère*, No. 3, 1957, p. 287 et seq., especially pp. 299 and 300. "Technical assistance can be of infinitely greater importance to underdeveloped countries than financial assistance." (p. 300).

[2] The Ogooué Mining Company (which will exploit the manganese of Franceville in the Gaboon) and the Fria Company (which exploits certain bauxite deposits in Guinea) have made themselves responsible for a large part of the basic economic installations which they need; the Bauxites du Midi company (which will exploit other bauxite deposits in Guinea) has made itself responsible for these in their entirety.

conditions. There is a growing international awareness of the truth of this statement; it is realized more and more that the idea of developing underdeveloped areas wholly or mainly through private initiative is just a dream. Moreover, true though it is that private capital played a larger part than public capital in international investment several decades ago, it should not be forgotten that it was largely used to finance state loans or the basic public services in the underdeveloped countries, so that it might be said to have been public capital which started off as private capital.[1]

On the other hand, it is very true that an effort by the nation itself is also indispensable; this was the theme of Chapter VIII. But in most cases the national effort is bound to be insufficient, and will have to be seconded by public aid from outside. This, however, is not all. The national effort and external aid do not simply exist side by side; there is a certain causal relationship between them.

This can be seen if we look at the particular case of the African countries where French is spoken. If, for each of the post-war years, the total amount of investment is compared with the amount of investment financed by public capital emanating from France, there is seen to be a remarkably constant proportion of 3.2 between the two figures.[2]

If aid from Metropolitan France increases, other sources of finance, i.e. mainly public and private effort in the countries affected themselves, increases also; if it decreases, a decrease in the other investments is also noticeable. This relationship is both visible in the overall figures, and can be observed in operation in any given situation. Whenever a region is cleared or irrigated or a road opened, almost immediately plantations are laid out,

---

[1] cf. Chapter X, p. 107.
[2] These figures were calculated for thirteen overseas countries (French West Africa, French Equatorial Africa and the Cameroons). The proportion of 3.2 is constant in time but not in space (the true figure is higher in some of the countries in question, and lower in others); it is therefore an average figure. The calculations were made by Monsieur Maldant of the Directorate of Economic Affairs and Planning in the Ministry of French Overseas Territories.

smaller works are completed and houses built. Local investment is responding to investment from Paris by the operation of a multiplier. It may not be true, as is too often said, that public investment from France represents practically all the investment there is in the African territories (as we shall see, it accounts for less than one third); nevertheless, it unquestionably plays a vital, because a dominant and an inductive, part.

It is also said that the large public contribution made by Metropolitan France is counterbalanced by large withdrawal of private capital. But it would be superficial to conclude that the influence of the incoming capital is, to that extent, cancelled out. Even assuming an extreme case in which withdrawals of capital were exactly equal to the incoming assistance from public funds; still the latter would exert a considerable influence by a process which can be compared to the chemical phenomenon of catalysis, in which a substance enables a large reaction to take place although it emerges almost unchanged from the process. From this point of view the effect of public assistance seems to be rather similar to that of a monetary injection; it has a stimulating effect.[1]

Between foreign private investment on the one hand, and national savings on the other hand, public aid from abroad thus forms a fundamental bridge. But does it really perform this function in the world of today?

Scarcity of aid from public funds

We shall now try to estimate the amount given annually from public funds in assistance to underdeveloped countries, first under bilateral agreements, then in regional schemes of multilateral co-operation, and finally through worldwide organizations.

---

[1] This development does not of course mean that it is desirable for private capital to leave overseas countries in any quantity; on the contrary, it is most desirable that it should be re-invested locally and every encouragement should be given for it to do so. The intention was simply to point out the *static* mistake of judging the effect of external assistance by simply totting up the balance of payments. Only a *dynamic* view of capital movements gives a true idea of the consequences.

Bilateral assistance given by the countries of the West is shown in the table below (in thousand millions of dollars).[1]

Average	Bilateral gift	Bilateral loans (net)	Total of bilateral aid	Multilateral contributions	Total contributed from public sector
1950-1955	1.2	0.6	1.8	0.1	1.9
1956	2.0	1.0	3.0	0.2	3.3
1957	2.3	1.1	3.4	0.4	3.9
1958	2.7	1.4	4.1	0.4	4.5
1959	2.5	1.7	4.2	0.4	4.5
Average 1956-1959	2.4	1.3	3.7	0.3	4.0
1960	2.7	1.5	4.2	0.7	4.9

The following table, giving the assistance granted in 1960,[2] shows how the various Western nations contributed to the total effort :

Thousand million dollars.

Country	Gifts	New Loans	Gifts + New Loans	Multilateral Contributions
AUSTRIA	—	—	—	0.1
BELGIUM	86.0	—	86.0	12.9
CANADA	48.1	—	48.1	16.7
DENMARK	1.0	—	1.0	3.1
FRANCE	695.0	87.0	774.0	51.5
GERMANY	7.7	151.0	158.7	49.7
JAPAN	2.0	80.0	82.0	8.7
ITALY	8.9	19.4	28.3	12.1
NETHERLANDS	26.1	5.4	31.5	15.6
NORWAY	1.0	—	1.0	2.6
PORTUGAL	1.8	32.4	34.2	—
SWEDEN	1.0	—	1.0	5.7
SWITZERLAND	2.0	—	2.0	1.8
UNITED KINGDOM	165.0	183.7	348.7	45.5
UNITED STATES	1,481.0	854.0	2,335.0	235.5

[1] The next two tables show, in addition to bilateral assistance, national contributions to the multilateral assistance mentioned a little further on in the text.

[2] The above totals do not tally exactly with the figures in the preceding table; the main reason for this is that bilateral loans are shown net in the preceding table whilst gross amounts are given in this one.

The channels used by the United States for distributing its assistance are chiefly the Agency for International Development (AID),[1] the Export-Import Bank[2] and the provisions of the Agricultural Trade Development Assistance Act.[3] In the past, Asiatic countries have received the greater share of such assistance, but there has recently been a sharp increase in the amount granted to Latin America, whereas Africa and the Middle East have on the whole received little from the United States.

The two Western countries giving the largest amount of aid after the United States are France and Great Britain, in that order. Each of these countries gives a very large part of its aid to countries with which it has special links, and Africa is the principal gainer thereby.

It is very difficult to estimate how much aid is given by the USSR, because documentation on the subject is very scarce and, more importantly, because one can hardly ever be certain of the period covered by any given allocation of credits. With these reservations, one may hazard the guess that 300 million dollars would be a reasonable estimate of the value of assistance given by the USSR to its underdeveloped allies. This aid is all given in the form of loans at a very low rate of interest (2 per cent) but at fairly short term, 10 years being the maximum.

Turning to the assistance given by the USSR and its allies in China and Europe to underdeveloped countries which are not communist, we find that it averaged 516 million dollars per annum during the seven years 1954-1960; this figure does not include military aid (which averaged 174 million per annum). The value of aid increased noticeably during the latter part of the period, and economic aid seems to have totalled something like 1,000

---

[1] Since 1961 the AID has taken over the activities previously carried on by the International Co-operation Administration (ICA) and the Development Loan Fund. The programmes include gifts, loans and technical assistance.

[2] The Export-Import Bank makes loans both to governments and to private undertakings.

[3] Public Law No. 480. This law permits agricultural surpluses to be sold for payment in local currency. The local currency thus acquired can be used for various purposes, including loans and gifts for economic development.

million dollars in 1960. Geographically, it was divided as follows
over the seven-year period :

Asia	1608	(India 933, Indonesia 509)	
Middle East ...	1286	(Egypt 604, Afghanistan 217, Irak 216, Syria 179)	
Latin America	322	(Cuba 215, Argentine 104)	
Europe ...	116	(Yugoslavia 111)	
Total	3611	million dollars	

The aid was given mainly in the form of long-term loans at
low interest ($2\frac{1}{2}$ per cent). Repayment can be made, partially at
least, in local currency or in the form of exports. In certain ex-
ceptional cases China, and less frequently Russia, made gifts instead of loans. The aid was earmarked mainly for the execution
of large industrial, mining or transport schemes, and was much less
oriented towards agricultural development, education and health.

Thus, the very conjectural amounts which can be put forward
as representing the value of assistance given by communist countries to underdeveloped ones appear to have varied between
800 and 1,300 million dollars during the last few years.

This means that something over 5,000 million dollars' worth
of aid is given bilaterally each year from all sources.

A far smaller amount is given as multilateral aid. The figures
for aid given in connection with regional organizations have been
almost negligible up till now, whether through regional commissions of the United Nations,[1] various regional organizations outside the UNO[2] or even the Colombo Plan,[3] which seems to be a

[1] The Economic Commission for Latin America, the Economic Commission
for Asia and the Far East and the Economic Commission for Africa each have
available sums of the order of 1 million dollars a year, and thus are hardly
in a position to carry out any overall studies. Nevertheless, the Economic
Commission for Asia and the Far East does have a small technical assistance
programme.

[2] Caribbean Commission, South Pacific Commission, Technical Co-operation Commission for sub-Saharian Africa (CCTA). Hitherto these organisations
have been predominantly Western clubs, and their budgets amount only to
some hundreds of thousands of dollars a year, so that they can only carry out
general studies. In 1957, however, the CCTA did try to take on a new lease
of life by asking independent countries in Africa to become members and
by launching a sizeable technical assistance programme with the name of
FAMA (Mutual Assistance Fund in Africa south of the Sahara). This fund has
between 200 and 300,000 dollars a year.

In this connection two other regional organizations which make available mean for co-ordinating what in essence are bilateral measures.[1] On the other hand, the association with the European Economic Community of overseas countries linked to its member states has given rise to a considerable five-year programme for the period 1958 to 1962; by an annexe to the Treaty a fund which has an average annual income of 116 million dollars has been set up. In addition, the European Investment Bank, which is also an organ of the European Economic Community, is aiding Greece to the extent of 125 million dollars, spread over 5 years. Lastly, the Interamerican Development Bank, which was founded in 1960, made loans amounting to some tens of millions of dollars during 1961.

More is done by the world organizations. For instance the United Nations specialized agencies gave technical aid and other assistance valued at 285 million dollars in underdeveloped countries from 1956 to 1959 inclusive, or rather more than 70 million dollars a year on the average. The value of such aid in 1960 was 88.3 million dollars.[2]

In financial terms, the International Bank for Reconstruction

some technical assistance funds should be mentioned; the Organization of American States, and the OECD (Organization for European Co-operation and Development).

[3] This is an ambitious development plan, affecting almost all the countries on the Indian sub-continent and in South-East Asia, which was launched by Great Britain in 1950 and extended until 1966.

---

[1] It is organized very flexibly. It is rather like a club where the development programmes of the various interested countries are discussed in common, where lists are made of possible projects and of essential ones and where the best methods of execution are sought by comparing what is done in different countries. Apart from a technical co-operation bureau there is no permanent executive organ. The main organ is a consultative committee which has met once a year since 1950.

What the Colombo Plan in fact does is to co-ordinate and harmonize the efforts made by the Asian states concerned (who form 2/3 of the total), loans from the IBRD, to these countries, gifts and loans from the United States, and in the second place assistance coming from developed countries which have become members of the Plan (Canada, Australia, New Zealand, Japan and Great Britain). Britain gives mainly technical assistance, whilst also giving some loans and freeing the sterling balances held by these countries in Great Britain, which originate from orders placed by Britain during the Second World War.

[2] The following organizations or programmes were involved: UNEPTA. (United Nations Enlarged Programme of Technical Assistance), other technical assistance programmes of the United Nations, the U.N. Special Fund, the United Nations Works and Relief Agency (for Palestine refugees), and the UNICEF (United Nations International Children's Emergency Fund).

and Development alone has done much more than this. From 1956 to 1959 it disbursed an average of 232 million dollars a year, rising to 244 millions in 1960. It will be recalled that the IBRD, which was created at Washington in 1945 by the members of the United Nations, makes loans at fairly low rates of interest (from $3\frac{3}{4}$ to 6 per cent) either to member states or to borrowers guaranteed by member states, using its own capital and also loans placed on the money market (as well as the proceeds of rediscounting operations). Hitherto most of its loans have gone to Asian countries (mainly those belonging to the sterling zone) and to Latin American ones. It is to be expected that the International Bank will in future years finance many more projects in underdeveloped countries, both as a deliberate act of policy and also thanks to an increase in the resources available to it.

When considering the activity of the IBRD we should not forget that of its daughter institutions the International Finance Corporation (a total of 16 million dollars from 1956 to 1959 and 13 million dollars for 1960), and the International Development Association, founded in September 1960, which lent 101 million dollars during the first six months of its operations.

Altogether, the worldwide international organizations spend each year a little less than 500 million dollars.

In all, *the various public aid funds amount to less than 6,000 million dollars a year, and nearly nine-tenths of this sum is given or lent under bilateral arrangements.* This figure represents less than one-fifth of the minimum amount required yearly for investment in underdeveloped countries.[1]

Besides being quite insufficient, this amount is very unequally divided both in respect of donors and recipients.

Some of the developed countries such as Germany, Canada, Australia and New Zealand make relatively small contributions. Of the others, the United States, the USSR and Great Britain make an effort by no means comparable with that of France, having regard to their respective national incomes.[2]

---

[1] cf. Chapter VII, p. 74.
[2] cf. Table p. 99.

Nor is the money distributed among the recipients according to any objective criteria. Thus, for the period 1954-1957 under-developed countries received in public aid under bilateral or multilateral auspices an average of 2 dollars per inhabitant yearly; yet in fact certain countries received more than 5 dollars per inhabitant yearly (Bolivia, Jordan, Morocco, and french-speaking countries taken as a whole : some received more than 10 dollars (South Korea, Formosa, Cambodia and Tunisia) and some even more than 20 dollars (Laos, South Vietnam and Libya). In contrast, the countries in the Indian sub-continent, Indonesia and communist China received very much less than the average of 2 dollars per head per year in international aid.

Lastly, the preponderance of bilateral arrangements gives to most of these assistance programmes a political tinge which does not further their effectiveness.[1]

Principles of Reform

If the total annual investment in underdeveloped countries is to reach $30 thousand million, clearly public assistance must be increased far beyond its present level. To crystallize ideas, and without claiming any scientific basis for the figure, one might suggest that the present effort should be multiplied by at least two or three, to bring it up to $10-15 thousand million; and even this would be only one-third or half the amount needed.

There is nothing alarming about these figures when it is recalled that world military expenditure amounts to some $100 thousand million every year, for the necessary increase in public aid is only one-tenth of the total of military budgets. Contrasting these figures not only gives a useful comparison; it might even suggest a means of raising the money. Many people have already put forward the view that disarmament could be linked with aid to backward countries. Monsieur Edgar Faure is a strong exponent of this thesis.

Be that as it may, each developed nation will have to shoulder its share of the burden of expanding assistance towards equipping

[1] cf. Chapter XVI, pp. 180-182.

the underdeveloped countries.[1] An idea of what each one's share ought to be can be gained from a theoretical exercise. Let us imagine a kind of tax levied on all nations in which *per capita* incomes exceed $600 per annum, scaled according to the national revenue. These countries are the United States, Canada, Australia, New Zealand, Great Britain, France, Benelux, Germany, Switzerland and the Scandinavian countries. Let us also imagine that it was required to raise a total of $12 thousand million. Taking a proportional basis, the principal countries would have to pay the sums shown in the following table, as compared with public aid now given by these countries to the underdeveloped countries.[2]

If a system of progressive taxation were adopted, the United States would bear an increased burden because no other country has such a high *per capita* income. Other ways of dividing the load could of course be devised; one obvious course would be to lower the income threshold for taxable nations, thus bringing in further groups, including the USSR. This is unimportant for the moment. What matters is to demonstrate that many of the most highly developed nations should face the need for a radical increase in what they are doing for the underdeveloped ones.

	Annual National Revenue 1955-7 (in $000,000,000)[3]	% of Total	Proportional Contribution to World Tax (in $000,000,000)	Present Public Assistance to Underdeveloped Countries (in $000,000,000)[4]
UNITED STATES	347.8	64.1	7.69	2.57
GREAT BRITAIN	46.1	8.5	1.02	0.39
FRANCE	40.8	7.5	0.90	0.83[5]
GERMANY	35.1	6.5	0.78	0.20
CANADA	23.1	4.3	0.52	0.06
AUSTRALIA	10.3	1.9	0.23	0.05
OTHER COUNTRISS	38.9[6]	7.2	0.86	
TOTAL :	542.1	100.0	12.00	

[1] There are a number of signs that Germany has now decided upon a real contribution to the underprivileged nations, in the Middle East, in Black Africa and in Latin America.

[2] Table, p. 102.

[3] Source: U.N. Monthly Statistical Bulletin, December 1959.

[4] The figures in this column include sums given as bilateral assistance, plus the share taken in the programmes of international organizations. They do not, however, include private investment. (See on this point Chapter X).

[5] France is thus the country whose present performance is nearest to the assumed obligation under the system of global taxation imagined above.

[6] Of which Benelux 15.1, Scandinavia 15.3, Switzerland 6.0 and New Zealand 2.5.

But it is also important that the money in question should be wisely distributed among the various indigent countries. The way to achieve this, whilst at the same time cutting the political strings attached by the industrial nations to the aid they give, is to make such aid as far as possible multilateral. One day it may be possible seriously to consider collecting from the developed countries contributions such as those envisaged above, within the ambit of a world organization. At all events, it cannot be regarded as satisfactory that multilateral aid should form, as it does today, only one-tenth of the total of public aid. There can be no doubt that a great gulf exists, as things are at present organized internationally, between institutions that finance profitable projects (the International Bank and the International Finance Corporation) and those that offer studies and advice. (UNO). To cure the sickness of underdevelopment the international organizations offer on the one hand diagnosis and on the other hand therapy limited to the sphere of operations which bring an economic return. But what is to be done when (as most frequently happens) the diagnosis points to remedies that are *not* financially profitable? The idea of SUNFED[1] was played with for years, but it now seems to have been buried for good.[2]

But it is not enough even to increase the amount of aid, to divide it fairly and to administer it largely on a multilateral basis. It still must be put to effective use, and this means that it must not be deflected from its proper goal of investment and that it must be integrated into the development programmes of the countries receiving assistance.

Aid from public funds is always in danger of being sidetracked, for the recipient is strongly tempted to use it simply as working

---

[1] Special United Nations Fund for Economic Development.

[2] The SUNFED setback was partly counterbalanced in 1957 by the large increase in technical assistance credits which, as mentioned above, were raised to $100 millions. But still only studies are undertaken. (cf. Chapter XII, pp. 147 and 154-5).

Since the International Development Association was set up in 1960, it is to be hoped that this gap may be bridged in the coming years, if the organization develops sufficiently; the IDA grants loans which are repayable at least partly in local currency; the loan periods and rates of interest are also very advantageous.

credits. Strange though it may appear at first sight, this is not very difficult. But the risk is grave, because to do this is to turn curative aid into a mere palliative, attacking the effects of poverty but not its causes. All countries need to be firmly restrained from such actions. The giving nation owes the receiving one the further service of preventing it from wasting the gift. With this in mind, it has sometimes been held that assistance should be given in the form of loans rather than gifts, since a loan obliges the recipient in principle to make productive use of what he has received. Possibly a still more effective way would be for *the country or the international organization distributing the assistance to tie it to definite, approved projects.*

This tendency to degrade curative into palliative assistance is unhappily so strong that it is not easy to stand against it. In this respect the United States gave a useful lead during the Marshall Plan period by urging wiser counsels upon the European countries, blinded by their immediate problems and always tempted to sacrifice their basic equipment needs to them.

Furthermore, assistance should always be linked to a conscious effort on the part of the receiving country; it must not be simply thrown at it, but should be *received,* that is to say, welcomed by a positive act of the recipient. Aid which is simply doled out is likely to have few virtues—a defect from which much of the American aid to underdeveloped countries suffers.

The Philippines have received an avalanche of dollars,[1] but it has been of little use to them because they have not been trained to use it properly. One is reminded of the film by Marcel Lherbier and Jean Cocteau entitled *La Comédie du Bonheur* in which a millionaire who had escaped from an asylum was filled with the desire to do good to his neighbour. He began his programme by offering an incredible wad of banknotes to a poor man who promptly had a fit and passed out on the spot. The rest of the film showed that the millionaire had learnt his lesson and was using a different method; he was using his money to foster

[1] $760 million during the 10 years following the war, plus an almost equal amount in the form of a deficit on current account (for about 20 million inhabitants).

happiness by operations in which the beneficiaries could participate in mind, will and feeling. Backward countries can be developed only if the assistance they receive enables them consciously
to will their own development, and this fact has several implications.

It means firstly that countries which have a feudal structure
are not well placed to receive foreign aid, because it glides off
them like water off a duck's back. There must be a foothold
to enable development to get started; agrarian reform and the
setting up of co-operative institutions are essential prelim-
inaries.

Moreover, external aid must form part of a plan thought out
by the country itself.

Lastly, this collaboration by the receiving nation cannot be
merely intellectual; it must be willed, and this implies an effort;
in other words, foreign aid cannot be fruitful unless it is paralleled
by an effort from within the country. "Capital is made at
home".[1]

Even money received from abroad does not really become
capital, that is to say a productive element, unless it is desired
and willed as such "at home" and integrated in an effort made
by the nation. And there is nothing to prevent giving countries
from making their gifts conditional upon an effort by the receiving country itself. The function of foreign aid is not to replace
the nation's will but to be an agent in its effective mobilization;
whilst seeking to make it less cruel and less wedded to despotic
forms of power.

[1] NURKSE, *Problems of capital formation in underdeveloped countries*,
p. 141.

Chapter Ten

THE ROLE OF PRIVATE CAPITAL

ROUGHLY A third of the poor nations are within the Communist *bloc*, where the problem of private investment naturally does not arise. But other underdeveloped countries whose present political philosophy does not exclude private ownership of the means of production can envisage the use of private capital, especially from abroad, to hasten their growth.

There are two advantages in using private investments from abroad. Quantitatively it makes for a higher total volume of investment, supposing the nation's public effort and public assistance received from abroad to be at a given level. Qualitatively, when capital from abroad is invested directly[1] it is usually accompanied

---

[1] Direct investment means that the physical or legal person in country A, the investing country, exercises *de facto* or *de jure* control over the assets created in country B by means of the investment. The following are examples of direct investment: the formation in country B of a subsidiary of a company in country A or of a company in which a company in country A has a majority holding; the formation in country B of a company, which may legally be domiciled in country A, country B or even a third country, financed by capitalists in country A; or the building or purchase of fixed property situated in country B by nationals of country A.

Conversely, indirect investments are those not possessing the above characteristics; they consist mainly of transferable securities, representing a part of the assets in country B owned by nationals of country A (securities issued or guaranteed by the government of country B, debentures issued by a company in country B, or shares of a company in country B when these do not amount to a controlling share).

by human assets which put the material equipment to its best use. For whilst there is nothing absurd in the idea of publicly run industries, in the West it is private industry which provides a reservoir of men of the calibre to manage an industrial undertaking.

And yet private investment does not always have a good press in the underdeveloped countries (this was evident during the stormy journey of Mr. Nixon, then Vice-President of the United States, in Latin America in 1958. The influx of private capital was viewed not as a welcome action by the United States, but as an unwanted one).

For such investment is denigrated as aiming at enriching the capitalists, not at developing the country. The former is indeed the aim, and yet, without subscribing to the somewhat ingenuous notion of a natural harmony of economic interests, one may perhaps allowably take the view that a prosperous private undertaking usually contributes to the prosperity of the host country.

The export of funds to which it gives rise is also held against private investment. But as we saw in Chapter III, whilst it is difficult to avoid large payments of this kind, the amount of money remaining in the country as primary incomes is subject to a multiplier—sometimes quite a high one.[1] Besides, it is open to the state to take back some of these profits in the form of taxes if it thinks they are excessive, though its demands should be reasonable lest it dry up the very source of the income.[2] The state can also encourage the enterprise to re-employ its profits locally; to seek to freeze them within the country, however, would be self-defeating as it would simply frighten off other would-be investors.

Private investment from abroad is also blamed for constituting a sort of foreign body within the country's economy. This is indeed a real danger, though the dualist theory has perhaps painted the

---

[1] cf. Chapter III, pp. 35-39.

[2] With increasing frequency, the point of equilibrium between profits to be left to the company and the amounts to be taken by the state in taxation and other fiscal measures is being discussed before the investment takes place, while the financial agreement is being elaborated. (cf. Chapter III, pp. 31-32.)

picture a little too starkly, for it is in the interests of the state and of the foreign enterprise alike to make every effort to integrate the latter into the nation, and there are plenty of ways of doing this, given the will.[1]

A realistic view will seek to avoid two opposite mistakes, the first of which is to regard private capital as a panacea. Public investment, whether it comes from abroad or at home, is indispensable.[2] That is the weakness of the growth situation as it was in Latin America, at least until 1960, and it provides an excuse, if not a justification, for the anti-American utterances made in Latin-American countries. The ratio of 1 to 3 or 4 between public and private investment which is said to exist there is certainly not a healthy one.

It is however just as mistaken to entertain an exaggerated mistrust of private capital. The economic system prevailing in non-Communist countries has its advantages and disadvantages, and it would be foolish not to make full use of the advantages. It would, of course, be ridiculous to act as though any sort of private investments were suitable for any conditions. The Government should examine each case carefully and strive to obtain the terms most favourable for the state and the nation. But it does seem to be in the interest of the underdeveloped countries themselves to enter such discussions with the sincere desire to reach a favourable conclusion.

Since private investment in underdeveloped countries is a desirable thing, it is necessary to assess its present extent and to form an idea of the conditions and prospects for its development.

Movement of Private Capital to Underdeveloped Countries— the Present Situation.

The table overleaf shows the net annual amounts of new private loans and investments in underdeveloped countries, including reinvested profits (in thousand millions of dollars).

---

[1] cf. Chapter III, pp. 33-35 and 37-38.
[2] cf. Chapter IX, pp. 92-93.

Average 1950-1955	...	...	...	...	1.3
1956	...	...	...	...	2.4
1957	...	...	...	...	2.8
1958	...	...	...	...	2.2
1959	...	...	...	...	2.0
Average 1956-1959	...	...	...	...	2.4
1960	...	...	...	...	2.1

The greater part of these funds came from the United States, with Great Britain a good way behind, followed by France. For 1960 the figures are as follows (in millions of dollars): USA, 895, United Kingdom 436, France 182, Netherlands 171, Germany 110, Japan 86, Italy 82, Switzerland 79, Belgium 80.

The present figures for the United States are lower than those for 1956 and 1957. American private investments in underdeveloped countries were valued as follows : 1956, 1259; 1957, 1809; 1958, 914; 1959, 935; 1960, 895 million dollars. By far the largest part of this capital went to Latin America.

It is also noticeable that the greater part of Britain's outgoings represents net exports of new capital (373 million dollars out of 436 in 1960), whereas Germany's contribution consists mainly of long-term credits for expansion, and reinvestment of profits accounts for a large part of the outgoings from Belgium and the Netherlands. There is a special difficulty in obtaining reliable figures for France, since the funds in question go almost entirely to countries which are members of the franc zone, in the majority of which there is no check on capital movements to or from France.

All in all, it can be estimated that foreign private investments in underdeveloped countries are worth about 2,000 million dollars a year, which represents approximately half of all long-term exports of private capital.[1]

---

[1] The scale of these operations is not substantially altered if a proportion of the sums raised by the International Bank in the various money markets is added to the above figures. The Bank's activities are known to include the issue of bonds to the public and also the sale of credits, with or without its own guarantee.

It may be noted that these investments are largely direct, whereas before the second world war, and particularly before the economic blizzard of 1929, owners of capital in the developed countries usually subscribed to loans issued by the governments of underdeveloped ones, a form of investment which has since been considerably reduced.[1] The flow of private capital to the public sector of indigent countries has been replaced by public aid from industrialized countries to the public sector of the poorer ones. Nowadays private capital flows to the private sector of those countries.

The foregoing figures relate to net investment. Only operations in which the money is tied up for more than 5 years have been considered as investments, a criterion which eliminates nearly all the medium term credits given by private suppliers to countries which are being industrialized, whether or not such credits are guaranteed by banks and whether or not they are re-discounted by the issuing house or by governmental export credit guarantees in the supplier's country. Industrial countries give credits of this nature to the value of many hundred million dollars each year.

Such credits apart, private capital devoted to the backward countries amounts to about one fifteenth of their total investment needs according to the minimum which was calculated in Chapter VII. The total of private and public investments coming from abroad does not exceed 8 thousand million dollars, or about a quarter of the minimum needs.

Is this movement of private capital towards the underdeveloped countries likely to increase? We shall first look at existing trends, and then consider what incentives might be given.

The natural chances of private investment in the backward countries.

Investors can be attracted to underdeveloped countries by the hope either of purchasing raw materials or of selling capital goods or finished products.

---

[1] We should, however, note that British and Belgian territories still float large loans on the capital markets of their metropoli.

In reality, the basic motive is the search for raw materials. Of American investments abroad, those going to Canada and Western Europe are aimed at securing a foothold in the selling market, whilst those going to underdeveloped countries are essentially connected with supplies for the United States, especially of mineral products. Similarly the large private investment schemes in African countries within the French sphere of influence are all concerned with the production of raw materials (iron, manganese, bauxite and electrical energy).[1]

Nurkse thinks that from this point of view the nineteenth century was more favourable to the poor countries than the twentieth century.[2] There was in fact a boom in demand for raw materials during the nineteenth century owing to the expansion of population and the development of productivity in the West, and also because of Great Britain's decision to sacrifice its own agriculture to the international division of labour. Today, on the other hand, the United States, which is now the dominant country, acts in precisely the opposite way to Great Britain. Moreover, this is the era of synthetic products. There is less investment abroad because raw materials are not so urgently needed.

However, a careful examination shows that, contrary to Nurkse's opinion, industrial countries are being obliged by their need for raw materials to form ever closer links with underdeveloped ones. This remark applies particularly to mineral products, which with the exception of coal are found in much greater quantity in the underdeveloped countries than in others, and is especially true of bauxite, iron ore, oil and hydroelectricity.

Before the Second World War bauxite production was mainly in the hands of the big industrial countries, but today these have taken second place to the underdeveloped ones. Jamaica, British Guiana and Surinam alone produce 10 million tons a year out of a world total of 19 million tons.[1] Intensive search has been going

---

[1] On electrical energy as a raw material see below, p. 115.
[2] NURKSE, *Problems of capital formation in underdeveloped countries*, p. 87.

on in the world for bauxite deposits, since the demand for bauxite which is linked with aluminium production increases by at least 100 per cent every ten years; these researches have shown that the large producing centres in the immediate future will probably be the region of the Antilles and the Guianas, Guinea (all of which are underdeveloped countries) and a completely underdeveloped desert area in Australia facing Papua.

At present, production of iron is still largely in the hands of the big industrialized countries. Of the world total of 400 million tons the United States produce 100, the USSR 70 and France 50, the other important producers being Sweden, Great Britain, Germany, Canada and only one underdeveloped country, namely China. But what will be the position tomorrow? The United States, the USSR, France, Germany, Great Britain and Sweden expect to increase their production by only moderate amounts. The expansion of world demand for iron will undoubtedly be met partly from the considerable progress which is expected in Canada; but new producers, all of which are underdeveloped countries, will also enter the field. These will include Latin American countries such as Brazil and Venezuela, countries in the Sahara or south of it (Gabon, Liberia, Sierra Leone, Mauretania and Sahara) or finally India. It is not at all unlikely that Latin America and Black Africa may be producing several tens of millions of tons by 1975—possibly about 40 millions, or even more. This might well be the beginning of a new period of prosperity for such countries. The great steel-producing concerns of the world, especially the American, German and British ones, are keenly interested in Brazil, Africa and India; it may be that these countries contain the world's largest reserves, from which the needs of the twenty-first century will be supplied.

It is not by chance that the tropical countries are the most important ones where future supplies of aluminium and iron are concerned. These two metals are very widely distributed beneath

[1] The other large producers are three underdeveloped countries (Yugoslavia 0.9 million tons, Greece 0.9 and Guinea 0.6) and various other developed or semi-developed countries (United States 1.4, France 1.7, Hungary 0.9, USSR 1.1).

the earth's surface, but can be economically exploited only where there is a sufficient concentration. Now it happens that in the tropical zones the heavy rains dissolve and carry off the compounds of calcium, phosphorus and silicon, and tend eventually to leave iron oxide and aluminium oxide in relatively greater concentration.[1] In this way they act as selective agents, filtering the iron and aluminium by eliminating impurities, and thus doing some preliminary work for mankind so that bauxite, and to a smaller extent iron, can be described without exaggeration as truly tropical products. Whether the rainfall has this effect because of its intensity or of its relatively high nitric acid content, or because it is combined with high temperatures, who knows? But the fact is undeniable.

Now iron and aluminium seem to be the two basic metals of the modern age. Mankind has been interested successively in various metals as he has learnt to overcome the increasing difficulty of isolating them, particularly of separating them from oxygen; the first non-ferrous metals to be used were those which are easiest to reduce : then came iron, and later still aluminium. That is why the bronze age came several thousand years before the iron age[2] and the aluminium age three thousand years after the iron age.[3] When one looks at the rate at which metal is being used in the twentieth century and will doubtless be used in the twenty-first century it seems that the supply of non-ferrous metals, which are not found too abundantly in nature, will be less and less sufficient for the needs of mankind. Iron and aluminium, on the other hand, are basic constituents of geochemistry.[4]

As regards oil, the following table gives the relative importance

---

[1] One form which this takes is the phenomenon, well-known in Africa, of lateritization.
[2] It seems certain that the iron age began in Armenia about 1400 BC. The knowledge of ironworking has spread slowly, and indeed parts of the earth have not yet reached the iron age.
[3] A century ago in Western Europe.
[4] It is not by chance that the symbols for iron and aluminium are found in the names given by geologists to two of the great divisions of the world : Nife and Sial.

of the main producers with respect to production and known reserves.

	PRODUCTION 1960		KNOWN RESERVES	
	In Millions of Tons	%	*In Thousand Million Tons*	%
Middle East	257	23.8	24.6	61.2
of which : Kuwait	81	—	—	—
Saudi Arabia	61	—	—	—
Iran	51	—	—	—
Irak	47	—	—	—
North America less Mexico	408	37.8	4.7	11.7
of which : United States	382	—	—	—
Latin America	193	17.9	3.3	8.2
of which : Venezuela	149	—	—	—
Mexico	14	—	—	—
Non-Communist Asia	27	2.5	1.2	3.0
Western Europe	15	1.4	0.4	1.0
Africa	14	1.3	1.0	2.5
Communist world	165	15.3	5.0	12.4
of which : USSR	146	—	—	—
WORLD TOTAL :	1,079		40.2	

Leaving aside the Communist countries for which we have few reliable figures, the present production of underdeveloped countries in the Middle-East, Latin America, Asia and Africa is just about exactly equal to that in developed ones, namely North America minus Mexico, and Europe. This is a recent phenomenon brought about by the very large increase in production in the Middle East and Venezuela since the war. In 1938 the Middle East was still producing only 15 million tons and Venezuela 28 million, amounting at that time to 5 and 10 per cent respectively of total world production.

If we now look at the figures for known reserves, we see that underdeveloped countries account for 75 per cent of the world total and 86 per cent of the non-communist world share. Moreover, it seems likely that the relative importance of the Middle East (an underdeveloped area) will increase considerably. Whereas present-day production in the area is about equal to that in Latin America, the known reserves are eight times larger.

Beyond known reserves stretches the shadowy terrain of reserves whose existence is presumed or hoped for; among these the Sahara, another underdeveloped territory, is a prominent focus of attention. Apart from the material raw materials—if one may so describe them—just mentioned, electricity is truly a non-material raw material. For those branches of industry which are generally known as electro-industry it is a basic element in costs of production. The various branches of the electro-industry, such as aluminium, ferrous alloys, and phosphorus industries, as well as the isotopic separation of uranium which are rapidly increasing in importance among modern industries, need a great deal of electricity, and cheap electricity at that.

Owing to the abundance of tropical rainfall the most powerful rivers are generally to be found within the tropical zone. It is no accident that the two greatest hydo-electric projects now being planned are both situated in the tropics—that of Inga in the Congo (34 million Kw) and that of the Owen Stanley Range (15 million kW) in Papua, facing Australia and under her sovereignty.

The tropical zones generally are rich in potential sources of power. This is true of the Indian sub-continent and above all of Black Africa, which has the largest area within the heavy rainfall zone, that is to say between the 15th parallel north and the 10th parallel south, and which moreover has pivoted on its quaternary strata in such a way as to create sharp differences of level close to the Atlantic. Experts believe Africa to be endowed with about half the world's hydro-electric potential and the price per kilowatt-hour is strikingly low. Leaving aside Scandinavia, a marginal kilowatt-hour (i.e. produced from the most efficient dam which can now be constructed) in Europe costs $\frac{2}{3}$d; in North America it costs approximately $\frac{1}{4}$d. With dams like that at Sanaga in the Cameroons, of Konkouré in Guinea or of Kouilou in Central Congo[1] the price is nearly down to 1/5th of a penny—rather more for Konkouré, but much less for the two others.

This hydro-electric power can be utilized for any type of industry using electricity. The Kariba dam on the Zambesi river in Rhodesia, which develops 800,000 kW mainly serves the copper industry. Kouilou and Inga, on the other hand, are largely designed for a group of industries based on aluminium, ferromanganese, ferro alloys, cellulose and possibly isotopic separation. But many of these projects are designed primarily with the aluminium industry in view, and in this connection the fact that bauxite is very often found close to hydro-electric power in the tropics will determine the sites of many of the great industrial installations of the near future. The Caribbean, which has little power, has to send its bauxite to the United States or Canada for processing by hydro-electric power, but it is probable that the bauxite of Guinea will be transformed into aluminium[2] in Black Africa itself with the help of the Sanaga,[3] Konkouré, Kouilou and Congo dams. Similarly, the Owen Stanley range will transform the bauxite of Queensland in Australia and Malaya's bauxite will be treated in Sumatra. These are destined to be the great industrial centres of the aluminium industry before very long. Thus the underdeveloped world, and particularly those parts of it which are in the tropics, now have a piece of unexpected good fortune; for whilst development cannot consist of mining alone, or even of mining plus industry, it can receive a considerable impetus from them.

Underdeveloped countries sometimes look with disfavour on projects aimed at supplying their raw materials to the industrial world at large. It is natural that they should prefer to set up industries which will produce goods for local consumption. But the

[1] Giving respectively 150,000, 450,000 and 750,000 kW.

[2] To speak more accurately, bauxite is first transformed into alumina which is then transformed into aluminium by electrolysis.

[3] This dam, which is completed, supplies the Péchiney-Ugine aluminium company's factory in the Cameroons (ALUCAM), which has an annual capacity of 50,000 tons of aluminium.

two are not mutually exclusive; on the contrary the money brought in by the large mining undertakings can also accelerate other forms of industrial investment.

It is also legitimate for the countries which produce raw materials to want the processing to be done locally. This should certainly be the aim wherever it can be done. Moreover, one of the raw materials we have just mentioned, namely electricity, will have to be used locally because it is very wasteful to transport it for really long distances. Electrical energy, in fact, makes possible the local treatment of other raw materials; as we have seen, the chances of processing minerals where they are found depend very often upon the availability of electrical potential.

There are, however, certain cases in which local processing of raw materials is not practicable because it cannot be done economically. When the local government has assured itself beyond reasonable doubt that this is so it will be well advised to sanction projects which, even if they do not involve local processing, will at least bring in extra revenue to the state. Besides this, such projects also indirectly help the nation's overall development either by training industrial labour, the existence of which may then attract further investment, or by virtue of the roads, railways and energy supplies which, although built in the first place for the benefit of the project in question, can at the same time be useful to other branches of the national activity. For example, a dam built for the use of a certain large industrial project using electricity may also enable other light industrial undertakings to be set up, or add to the amenities of private life in the district. In the same way, railways such as those which have been built for the Mauretania iron mines (now under construction) and those of Mekambo in Gabon are bound indirectly to assist other forms of development within the country.

Thus through possessing some of the raw materials most in demand in the industrialized countries, underdeveloped ones have a chance which should be seized all the more eagerly because it may not last indefinitely. For how many decades will the heyday of tropical dams last when the nuclear era really begins? How much longer are iron and aluminium destined to dominate our civilization? When will they be replaced by other metals—by magnesium for instance, which can be obtained from sea water, or by other non-metallic substances? The tropics have before them perhaps a quarter of a century which will be very favourable to their industrial development; but it is by no means certain that they have much longer.

The search for raw materials attracts private investment. So also does the search for outlets. Developed countries may be seeking in the backward ones not only opportunities to purchase, but also the chance to sell either capital goods (on setting up the enterprise) or consumer products which the business itself may produce.

The wish to sell essential equipment or to carry out work associated with the project is one of the factors which persuade industrial groups to invest money in a project. For example, the shareholders of large mining undertakings in Black Africa include many who decided to participate because they hoped that either they themselves or businesses having close financial connection with them would be able to effect sales of considerable magnitude in supplying the project in question. However, groups interested only for reasons of this kind usually tend not to invest but to extend long-term credit to the purchaser, often of as much as five years' duration. Such credit procedures, usually helped by the government of the suppliers' country through guarantees and rediscount facilities, are very widely used by the industrialized countries supplying equipment to underdeveloped ones.

This method undoubtedly has disadvantages, since the underdeveloped country cannot always produce the talent for the proper functioning of the undertaking which was built by foreigners. This sometimes results in the latter being held responsible for unfortunate happenings which are in no way connected with the quality of the goods supplied. The French have been blamed, for instance, for some of the disappointment experienced in the working of the steel works at Paz del Rio in Colombia.

This has led industrial groups supplying equipment to try to evolve a more complex formula which includes both the construction of the factory and a technical assistance agreement covering a number of years to enable it to be given a proper start. Such a formula has been used by French industrialists in connection with the steelworks at Chimbote in Peru, a fact for which the lesson of Paz del Rio was directly responsible.

But even if the responsibility of a counsellor be added to that of a supplier, this still does not add up to the responsibility held by the manager of the undertaking himself. Contrary to the notion often held in underdeveloped countries it is much more to their advantage, though in certain respects perhaps less flattering, to attract foreign investment rather than the sale of goods and services on credit. For by so doing they stand to benefit from the assistance of competent business men in making the enterprise work and giving it connections with similar undertakings throughout the world, all of which materially assists the sale of its products. Moreover, once he has taken the plunge the foreign investor very often decides to plough back his profits locally, or even to transfer fresh capital to the underdeveloped country from the parent company, not necessarily because the enterprise is doing badly but quite possibly because it is doing very well, thus encouraging its founders to expand it still further.

Foreign investments aimed at setting up companies whose products can be sold on the local market are unhappily least frequent in the most underprivileged countries, as investors are discouraged by the small requirements of the market. Not until development has got under way is investment of this type likely to be made owing to the gradual appearance of effective demand with rising incomes. It is only since 1920 that foreign private money has been directly invested in Japan in any appreciable quantity; the first phase of development was financed by national savings or foreign loans, and also with the help of Western technicians; but the impetus came from the state. Brazil is just about to enter the stage at which foreign private investment can be attracted, and the Ivory Coast will in all likelihood be the first french-speaking country in Africa to reach it.

There is however one way in which the process can be hastened. When a foreign industrial undertaking has a predominant position as a supplier of an underdeveloped country it is in its own interests to take the initiative in industrializing the country as soon as a local factory becomes, even marginally, an economic proposition. For this metamorphosis gives it a chance of continuing to dominate the local market. Some branches at least of French industry would be well advised to follow this policy in french-speaking African countries.

It may be objected that to do this is to compete with oneself. But this objection does not apply if consumption of the product is growing or is likely to grow soon in the country in question. The choice before the parent company is then to extend its productive potential within the foreign market itself rather than within the country of origin; it is a policy of *transferred extension*.

Moreover, it is only necessary initially to arrange for the final stages of manufacture to take place in the underdeveloped country such as assembly for cars and cycles, conditioning for pharmaceutical products and hydration and bottling for concentrates. This transfer of activities frequently has solid technical advantages, because very often the last stage of the manufacturing process involves a considerable increase in the weight or size of the product, and generally speaking only a small investment is required to secure a considerable increase in value. Furthermore, whilst the parent company may lose an outlet for its finished products, it consolidates its outlet for its semi-finished products, i.e. at the penultimate stage. There is also the point that in so far as the local factory is not able to supply the whole of its market for finished products it will be the more ready to order the balance of its requirements from the parent company. It would on the whole be a mistaken policy for governments to oppose the installation of factories of this type, since it very often happens that having once arranged for the last stage to be done locally the parent company is gradually compelled willy-nilly to add the other stages by a process of vertical integration.

Finally, transferred extension can in certain cases lead to the transfer of the parent company's partly used tooling. This both speeds modernization of the parent company's plant considerably and also lowers the cost of setting up a factory in the underdeveloped country.[1]

Incentives by the host nation.

Governments of underdeveloped countries wishing to attract private investment should not rely solely on the natural chances of such investment which have just been analysed. They should take positive measures to encourage investors, and we shall see more clearly what form these encouragements should take if we first look at the obstacles which may discourage investors from placing their money in such countries. Some of these are purely economic whilst others, though having an economic element, are essentially political.

First there are the factors tending to increase production costs in underdeveloped countries, such as a lack of basic services—transport, power and public utilities, which often compel the head of a business enterprise to provide these facilities himself. Then comes distance from supplies, particularly of raw materials, resulting in high transport costs and necessitating larger stocks of spare parts, with the ever-present danger that time may be lost because a needed spare or a skilled worker is not available. There is also the absence of a pool of workers with industrial experience, so that even if wages are somewhat lower than elsewhere the work done is liable, initially at least, to be of poor quality. It thus becomes necessary to import not only management personnel but even skilled workers, with all the additional costs that this implies.

What may be called the economical-political obstacles are even worse. They may be summed up under the general heading of threats to stability. Fiscal instability is one of the most formidable of these obstacles.[2]

But operating conditions other than those concerned with taxation may also be unstable—social legislation, exchange control,

---

[1] On the question whether the most modern machinery is needed for industrializing underdeveloped countries, cf. Chapter XII, p. 137.
[2] cf. Chapter III, p. 32.

money and the foreign exchange market. And the ultimate risk is that of being despoiled through nationalization not tempered by proper compensation, or simply because, with or without the consent of the government,[1] operating conditions in general become so unsatisfactory that there is nothing left to do but close the business.

This latter risk is the investor's worst nightmare, especially since the confiscation of foreign savings in Latin America, Asia, and, even more spectacularly, in the Middle East. The events of Suez in 1956 undoubtedly had a bad psychological effect on the international capital market. Obviously the first concern of a capitalist is not to lose his capital.[2]

To encourage investors, the host nation must do its best to reduce difficulties of this kind.

Governments can best try to reduce the impact of factors tending to raise production costs by a sustained investment effort to provide adequate public utilities. Similarly, they can overcome the lack of indigenous trained workers by expanding the provision of technical instruction. But this in itself will not completely overcome the handicaps peculiar to underdeveloped countries and therefore governments must put into effect, at least for an interim period, some specific measures of support and relief.

The most obvious supports are fiscal advantages, such as tax freedom for a certain period after the investment, budgetary grants, or credits conceded on favourable terms both of interest and duration.

Protective measures would consist mainly of tariffs or import

[1] It is possible for an underdeveloped country to make life impossible for a foreign undertaking without actually wishing to do so, by thinking that it can go on indefinitely aggravating operating conditions in order to get money for its budget, for the workers or for some other beneficiary, thus killing the goose that laid the golden eggs. But the goose may also be killed knowingly, particularly in Asia; efforts have been made on occasion to discourage Western capitalists without officially proscribing them by making difficulties in regard to the transfer of money, exchange rates or taxation.

[2] The Dourdin Institute got the following replies to a questionnaire on what savers expected of their investments: anonymity 4 per cent, interest 23 per cent, liquidity 24 per cent, security 59 per cent.

quotas levied on competing products coming from abroad. Nevertheless, the promise or even the existence of such protection will not by itself sway the investor. For one thing, a protected market has to be large to be attractive. This consideration may suggest a policy of customs union, since a group of states might offer attractions which they could not give individually. It may thus be advantageous for underdeveloped countries to combine either among themselves or with countries which are already developed.

Underdeveloped countries may, then, combine to form larger economic units; but this alone is not enough. China abolished all provincial customs charges (known as "likin") in 1928, but this did not promote industrialization. Nevertheless, the creation of relatively large customs units can be a decisive factor in development, and the separatist tendency noticeable in many young countries beginning their development is thus particularly regrettable. Although some observers consider this to be inevitable, it must be said that if for example the territories formerly comprising French West Africa become "balkanized", their development is bound to be retarded in consequence.

To associate within one customs union or free trade area both underdeveloped and developed countries is naturally a more complex operation. On the one hand the industrialization of the underdeveloped country necessitates some protection by tariffs or quotas against external competition, including that from the developed country which is the partner in the customs union or free trade area. For example, in the french-speaking countries certain sectors of industry have to be protected from competition by France herself. Nevertheless, there is no doubt that membership of a large area which includes the extensive market of a developed country can be the means of attracting a considerable amount of investment. For example, in the history of Canada's rapid development Imperial Preference induced capitalists from the United States to gain entry into the preference area, and in particular the British market, by setting up factories in Canada. In the same way, many investment schemes now under way or planned within African countries belonging to the franc area are motivated at least in part by the possibility which this offers to foreign groups of obtaining free access to the French market.

But in so far as insecurity is the main hindrance to investment, official guarantees offer the means whereby the governments of backward countries can do most to attract private investment.

Long term tax arrangements were mentioned above.[1] Firm arrangements are advantageous in other spheres too, as witness what the Middle Eastern countries are doing in their oil agreements. Since 1956 it has been possible to make long term agreements in the African countries belonging to the French Community, and such measures are certainly desirable in order to reassure investors. Pushed to the extreme, this formula would lead to the reappearance of chartered companies (a second reappearance because, after having flourished during the seventeenth and eighteenth centuries, the idea was reborn in Africa towards the end of the nineteenth century). But such a system does not meet the political requirements of today. To say to a business undertaking : "Whatever the government of the country may decide in future, this will not apply to you" is psychologically dangerous, and we have already analysed[2] the serious disadvantages of allowing it to be thought that foreign businesses enjoy extraterritorial rights.

Apart from specific undertakings given to a company for a certain operation, more general safeguards applicable to all future investments, can be imagined. In 1949 the International Chamber of Commerce at its meeting in Quebec approved an international code of fair treatment for foreign investments. In 1951 the Swiss Banking Association proposed that an international agreement for the protection of private property should be concluded, and the events of Suez and Cuba have made this suggestion a very pertinent one. Many persons and groups have since taken up the idea of an international agreement, in particular Herr Abs[3] and M. Piaton[4] in France, in the context of the European Common Market.

[1] cf. Chapter III, pp. 31-32.
[2] cf. Chapter III, pp. 35-38.
[3] President of the Deutsche Bank.
[4] Chairman of Péchiney, died in 1958.

All these schemes and their variants are based on the idea of a charter for foreign investments which governments should be invited to sign. This charter would include a code of "fair practices"; identical treatment of foreign investments with investments by nationals of the country concerned; equal taxation of undertakings run on foreign capital with those run on capital owned by nationals; the same treatment and the same legal and judicial protection for foreigners as for nationals as regards their persons, goods, rights and interests; no discrimination as regards the nationality of shareholders, the choice of managers, the recruitment of administrative or technical personnel or managers; freedom of transfer for current payments on investments, or the reimbursement of principal, and for payments in respect of the maintenance and renewal of assets; facilities for the transfer within a reasonable period of money arising from the sale of assets or shares, and permission to effect such transfers in the currency of the creditor or in any other currency previously agreed between the debtor and the creditor; and, should nationalization take place,[1] fair compensation agreed before expropriation and transferable into the country of origin at the rate of exchange ruling on the day of expropriation. Cases not foreseen by this code would be submitted to arbitration.[2]

Lastly, there is the problem of ensuring that the arbitrator's decision would be carried out. There exists no means of compelling a State to execute on its own territory a judgement against itself. But if the dispute concerned a business producing exportable goods, then once they had left the country such goods could be a surety. This question raises delicate legal problems, which some eminent specialists have recently been studying.[3] These difficulties are not insurmountable if states agree to renounce the advantages they have in being immune from jurisdiction and

[1] Some drafts include an undertaking not to nationalize the business for a certain period.

[2] As regards the competent jurisdiction, some drafts propose the Permanent Court of International Justice at The Hague; but as this court can deal only with disputes between States, this hardly seems to be the right answer.

[3] Particularly in a meeting at Aix-en-Provence which was organized in May 1958 by the *Association de Droit Minier et Petrolier.*

from normal enforcement procedures. It may be added that the matter is simplified when the goods in question are sold f.o.b.; and there should be suitable publicity to discourage sellers in bad faith, and the right of recovery and of seizure from third parties acting in bad faith.

If, however, a group of developed and underdeveloped countries agreed to become signatories to an international convention of the type just described, any signatory which then went back on its word would be risking its good reputation *vis-à-vis* all the other signatories, not to speak of possible sanctions.

Nevertheless, too much reliance should not be placed on the safeguards conferred by such undertakings, especially when the currents of international politics disturb them. If he wishes to safeguard his money, the investor himself must be prepared to assess the good faith and the substance of the other party in relation to strains which the situation might place upon the contract later.[1]

International assistance towards the development of private investment.

Private investment can be assisted by international organization as well as by territorial governments, both by measures of financial support and by guarantees. It is often associated with aid given by developed countries or international bodies to underdeveloped countries in the form of gifts or loans;[2] in fact, such aid is some times a *sine qua non* of private investment. For example, the International Bank and its daughter institution the International Finance Company encourage private investment by granting loans on relatively favourable terms to new companies formed with private capital. In the same way, the F.A.C. (Assistance and Co-operation Fund) and the Central Bank for Economic Co-operation assume part of the financing of projects initiated by private capital in french-speaking countries, by the grant of gifts or loans. The Export-Import Bank, too, readily grants loans to subsidiaries

[1] cf. Chapter XIII, pp. 157-8.
[2] cf. Chapter IX, pp. 94-98.

of American companies which operate in underdeveloped countries.

In addition to this marriage between public and private investment, industrialized countries can encourage private investment in underdeveloped countries by the grant of various specific advantages to exporters of capital. At present, however, this is not much done, (if we except double-taxation agreements and credits granted to capital goods exporters by banks—often State-financed —specializing in this type of business).[1] Incentives of this type are not much in vogue except within certain politico-economic units such as the countries having special links with France.[2]

There is little likelihood of the rapid adoption of such policies by developed countries acting alone. Yet it may be hoped that a number of nations may agree upon a common policy comprising some such incentives. Thus it has been suggested that part of the credits held by the European Economic Community for the purpose of financing overseas countries should be used to supplement the interest paid on loans issued in the money market, thus obtaining much larger sums for the development of overseas countries.

With regard to guarantees, the industrialized countries have set up procedures covering commercial transactions with other countries, whether developed or not. In some countries such as Great Britain, Switzerland and the Scandinavian ones these are run by the government itself, either through special institutions in the running of which the state participates (as in Germany, Belgium and Italy) or under a mixed arrangement in which the decision rests partly with the government and partly with a private organization (as in the Netherlands and France).[3] In the United States the Export-Import Bank as well as making loans, is en-

[1] We saw above (p. 119) that investment should not be confused with the export of capital goods.

[2] Compare in particular the tax advantages granted in metropolitan France by the decree of 13th November 1956 to finance companies for the development of the overseas territories; to Algerian development companies by the decree of 31st January 1958; and to companies for the development of the Sahara by the order of 18th December, 1958.

[3] In France the organization in question is the *Compagnie Française d'Assurance pour le Commerce Extérieur* (COFACE).

titled simply to give its guarantee : but in spite of the attachment shown by the Republican administration to this formula for some time past, it has been little used.

But although considerable use is made of such mechanisms, at least by the industrialized countries of Europe, they are designed to guarantee commercial operations, not financial ones, a large proportion of the risks covered concerning payment for the sales of consumer goods. Other risks covered are those of the manufacturer who supplied the capital goods, but not of the actual investment made by the group which buys them.[1]

Moreover, the maximum period for which such credits are granted is very strictly limited, usually to five years.[2] In any event, the practice of guaranteeing commercial credits nowadays plays an important part in the sale of capital goods to underdeveloped countries, and many hundred million dollars are lent every year under such procedures.[3]

But could not the governments of industrialized countries, together with international organizations, jointly take the further step of guaranteeing the investment itself ?

Little has been done along these lines so far. The two main points to notice concern the United States and Germany respectively. In the United States, the Agency for International Development, like the organizations which have preceded it since the beginning of the Marshall Plan in 1948, is entitled to guarantee private investments. Very little use was made of this facility for a long time, especially as regards investments in under-

[1] See above, pp. 119-120 on this important distinction.

[2] For some time the Export-Import Bank in the United States has been able to go beyond 5 years, and little by little European countries in their turn are taking powers to grant 7, 8 or 10 years; Great Britain was the first, followed by Italy. France and several other countries. In any event, all the national systems evince more flexibility in practice than in theory; the Berne Union, meeting place of the national organizations concerned with this problem, is trying to prevent the various nations from constantly outbidding one another and ending up with foolishly unrealistic terms.

[3] This kind of insurance really covers two quite different kinds of risk, handled in France by different institutions. There are normal commercial risks; in France COFACE deals with these for its own account. Then there are political risks, i.e. those dependent in some measure on action taken by the government of the receiving country. In France, these are covered by COFACE which in turn is guaranteed by the state. We are here concerned with this second class of risks.

developed countries, but the present tendency is to use it more often. Germany, too, is enabled by the budgetary law of 1959-60 to guarantee private investments.

France does not guarantee the investments made in overseas countries attached to her; nevertheless, finance companies for the development of overseas territories and companies in Algeria and the Sahara for development purposes not only enjoy tax advantages[1] but may also receive the guarantee of a minimum dividend. Many companies of the above type have already received such a guarantee from the Finance Ministry and are thus encouraged to invest overseas.

The International Bank is authorized to guarantee loans, but in practice does not do so. It does however readily arrange loans repayable in annual instalments, in some cases guaranteeing the transaction itself.

In view of the uneasiness which the attitudes of underdeveloped countries arouse in the minds of many capitalists, much good could be done by an extension of such services. But they are not without their dangers. Anything tending to transform private property abroad into public property, even though it be limited to guaranteeing the financial risk, whilst it diminishes the risk to private investors, is nowadays likely to increase the overall risk; for governments of underdeveloped countries usually have noticeably fewer scruples about robbing foreign governments than about expropriating private property. And why should the French be surprised at this? For however scrupulous they may be in relations between persons, they are often much less so in dealing with the State. Thus there is a danger that the governments of underdeveloped countries might have no qualms about confiscation on a State to State basis.[2]

[1] See above, p. 127 note 2.

[2] At the end of 1961, guarantees given by the AID or the organizations which preceded it since guarantees were permitted (in 1948) amount to a total of 688 million dollars, whereas during the first ten years of this period they reached only 206 million dollars. Since 1960 only investments in underdeveloped countries may have the benefit of this system; at present, rather less than half the guarantees which have been granted cover such investments.

This observation applies particularly to dependent territories which may one day be tempted to say: "You were the State, but now I am; State property is now my property."

Developed countries can, however, combine to minimize this risk by following a common policy; multilateral assistance is preferable to that given individually. A procedure for joint international guarantee of private investments by a number of developed nations, or better still by a number of developed and underdeveloped ones, might well have very beneficial results.

Much could be learnt about procedures suitable for such guarantees from the National State Contracts Fund, a French institution which in essence transforms private guarantees which are perfectly sound but not well known, (such as a government contract, a letter of intent, or a corporate guarantee) into a guarantee which is both simple and readily acceptable, namely its own signature. An "International Guarantee Fund" could likewise mobilize promises and guarantees given by an underdeveloped country in connection with a private investment scheme, by adding its own signature to the undertaking.

Such schemes can be envisaged as working either on a world basis or regionally. For example, part of the funds which the European Economic Community allocates for development in overseas countries could be used to back such a guarantee fund; in return the government of the receiving country might be required to adopt a fair charter for private investments.

Chapter Eleven

ELEMENTS OF A TECHNOLOGY
OF DEVELOPMENT

CAPITAL IS very necessary for development, yet by itself it is not enough; men and methods are needed in order to put it to work. The present chapter and the two following ones are concerned with the methodological and human aspects of development.

First we shall try to show in the present chapter by what general principles the governments of underdeveloped countries should be guided. Should economic investments or social investments take precedence? Should investment be directed preferentially towards agriculture or industry? Is development best carried forward by the simultaneous execution of a number of different projects, or by applying a more or less rigid plan? We shall try to answer each of these questions in turn.

Economic or Social

It is usual to contrast two kinds of investment in underdeveloped countries—economic investments, the object of which is to increase wealth, and social investments, the object of which is to increase well-being and culture. This as a reasonably clear distinction provided it is borne in mind that some investments are difficult to allocate (to which category for example do temporary lodgings set up near to a work site belong, or the piping of water to the bush?). But the distinction is quite important considering that, at any rate as a rough guide, an economic investment tends to lighten the nation's financial burden whereas a social investment tends to increase it. To build a road or a dam is to open the way to an increase in the national income and consequently in the capacity of the nation to pay taxes. To build a dispensary or a school, on the other hand, makes sense only if we then put a doctor or a school teacher inside them, and this of course implies the payment of a regular salary. So a social investment gives rise to further expense for the state, which is bound to fall upon its budget.

Some observers tend to push this analysis to extremes and maintain that it is inexcusable weakness to spend a large part of the investment budget of an underdeveloped country on the social projects. But this view neglects an important part of the problem, namely the *economic effects of social investment*.

The nation's health is a most important part of its capital. Lack of energy at work, too little drive and concentration, are all too common in underdeveloped countries. It is usual to attribute them either to the climate (not without reason) or to the flabbiness of the indigenous people (often unjustly); but in fact they are very often caused by bad sanitation, reinforced by the great social scourges, or perhaps undernourishment of the present generation or its predecessors. The same is true of education; from the simple benefits of primary education up to college and university standard, it increases human efficiency, provided only that it is well directed. Countries which are in process of being developed need skilled workers more than office managers, and engineers more than lawyers.

Social investment, then, can greatly affect the products and services available. But it has an equally noticeable effect upon demand, at least in underpopulated countries. Taking the underdeveloped countries in the franc area, if we examine on the one hand population density and on the other hand agricultural productivity per inhabitant, it will be seen that their variations are closely correlated, the countries with comparatively high productivity being also those of high-density population (the Antilles, Réunion, Comores and the Northern part of Algeria) whilst the countries with poor productivity are also the least populated ones (Guiana, Mauritania, Equatorial Africa, and the Sudan), with the tropical forest zone and Madagascar between the two extremes.

Observation throughout the various countries of Black Africa of the Peuhls or Foulbe races has also shown that their individual productivity varied with the density of their group in a given country.

The existence of adequate demand is in fact a more important factor in the economic activity of underdeveloped countries than is usually thought.[1]

It follows that if we improve sanitation, and increase the expectation of life, if we cut down maternal mortality and pathological sterility, we contribute to the economic development of the countries concerned (at least where they are below the demographic optimum) just as much as by economic investment, indeed possibly even more so. We should therefore beware of regarding social capital as a demagogic form of investment. Both social and economic capital should be developed side by side, though the precise proportion between them will naturally vary according to the requirements of the situation.[2]

Agriculture or Industry?

Industrialization is usually considered to be such a basic constituent of development that the two words are often used as if they were interchangeable. Certainly no developed country is without a large amount of industry; even the so-called agricultural ones such as Denmark, Australia or New Zealand employ less than half their labour force in agriculture.

The benefits of industrialization are undeniable. It goes far towards solving the problems of countries suffering from under-

[1] cf. Chapter VIII, pp. 87-88.
[2] In the African countries France has generally given one fifth of the credits of FIDES to the social sector and four fifths to the economic sector.

employment; and any diversification of production renders the national economy less vulnerable and provides the state with a firmer tax base. Moreover, the national revenue stands to benefit considerably if agricultural or mineral wealth is processed locally. Industrialization confers psychological benefits too in backward countries; the factory chimney is a success symbol, proving that the nation has come to terms with the modern world. This, then, is one more reason why industry should be brought to backward nations, quite apart from the strictly objective ones; if there is no factory chimney there will be a social complex !

And yet the development of backward countries must be based primarily on the expansion of their agriculture, and this for several reasons.

First of all, it is not enough simply to aim at increasing the total income of the nation; how it is divided is just as important. Development must not be thought of as the superimposing of various new industrial and urban complexes upon a rural economy which remains in its primitive state. A certain minimum of equity in the distribution of the increased wealth resulting from economic growth must be observed, and this can be done only if agricultural development is made an important objective in its own right.

Even if attention be directed to an increase in overall revenue rather than to its distribution, it remains true that this can usually be achieved at far less cost in agriculture than in other sectors of the economy. After all, agriculture is already in being, whereas the other activities have to be created *ex nihilo*. By raising productivity a little through the improvement of strains, a little more through better methods, then a little more by the use of fertilizers, and then some more by pest control, agricultural revenue can be increased within a few years by anything from 25 to 40 per cent.

It would often be found that the most efficient investment that could be made in a given country pound for pound, would be the intellectual investment of placing rural advisers in groups of villages—or even in each village if necessary—to teach correct cultural methods.

Finally, agricultural development must come first because industrialization itself presupposes a productive agriculture. The country that wishes to have towns and factories must first make sure of an agricultural surplus. At the time of the industrial revolution, British agriculture was very advanced, with a clear surplus for export.[1] It is also common knowledge how closely the industrial dynamism of the United States is linked with high agricultural productivity. As Monsieur de Jouvenel wrote:[2] "The United States became mechanized because it was a country of high wages, and these high wages were due to high productivity in agriculture." He adds: "It is quite stupid to seek to introduce mechanization through gifts from outside and to raise wages by decree, instead of using the natural method which is to increase productivity in food growing." The USSR may well have committed a planning error in going ahead with industrial development without paying enough attention to creating a buoyant agriculture, at any rate up to 1953. Industrial production in the Union increased threefold between 1929 and 1939 whilst the growth of agricultural production did little more than keep pace with the population increase, and this led to serious inflationary tendencies. Japan had a more balanced conception of growth, and Communist China also seems to be firmly set upon the road to agricultural development. In 1956 the Chinese government announced its intention of increasing agricultural production by 150 per cent in twelve years.

The relative positions of agriculture and industry in the economic development of a backward country naturally differ according to the demographic situation. An over-populated country has a labour force available at once to be used in industry, whereas less populous ones, and especially those which (like

---

[1] It has even been held that the turning point was the introduction of the turnip. (NURKSE, *Problems of capital formation in underdeveloped countries*, pp. 52-53). Once crop rotation had been improved in consequence, he says, agricultural productivity increased rapidly, freeing part of the rural labour force for capital formation: according to this view, the industrial revolution was fathered by an agricultural revolution.

[2] *Le développement des pays économiquement arriérés et les problèmes posés à la France*, a lecture given before the Study and Liaison Committee of the French Employers' Federation on January 10th 1957.

many in Latin America and Black Africa) are underpopulated, have a more urgent need to develop their agriculture first, so as to avoid the danger of inflation.

But the analysis needs to be carried further; to speak only of industry in general is an over-simplification. Which industry? Bettelheim[1] maintains that underdeveloped countries should not, as a rule, hesitate to build up basic industry and also industry manufacturing equipment goods. He also holds that the most modern equipment should be used wherever possible in setting up a given industrial undertaking. "Simply to expand the use of techniques giving a low level of productivity does not constitute a forward step in development."[2] It is to be feared that the view expressed on the above two points is too rigid. The determination at all costs to have an equipment industry right from the start of industrialization can very often be a costly gamble. Bettelheim is right in emphasizing that it is in the interest of backward countries to reduce the strain on their payments balances as far as possible by keeping the import of capital goods to a minimum. This is, of course, well worth doing, but if the method used causes the price of such goods to rise steeply this can have a disastrous effect on the economy in general, and also on the balance of payments. It would seem wise to avoid all preconceived ideas in the matter, and especially romantic notions about heavy industry. In industrializing themselves, underdeveloped countries should give all possible encouragement to the establishment of every sort of industry which is technically and economically feasible in the conditions prevailing in the country. Clearly, governments should not base their judgment of a project entirely on its financial profitability;[3] but economic profitability, that is to say its direct and indirect effects on the national product

---

[1] Compare particularly: Sous-développement et Planification, *Politique étrangère*, No. 3, 1957, pp. 296-8.

[2] ibid. p. 297.

[3] Questions of financial profitability may legitimately sway the decision where the proposed industry would be financed privately. Even then, however, governmental permission and the goodwill with which the undertaking is regarded and encouraged should be dependent upon its economic profitability rather than its financial profitability.

and its distribution, should be the deciding factor in the decision. If, examined from this point of view, the establishment of basic industries appears possible, so much the better. But this does not seem too likely to happen very often.

Turning to the other question, when a new industry is being established, should the aim be to equip it with the most modern installations, or is it better to look for equipment which can employ a large number of workers? Bettelheim's position on this question also seems to be too dogmatic. In an overpopulated country, it is preferable in principle to establish industries of low capital-intensity; since the amount of capital available is limited in any case, it is desirable to spread it as broadly as possible so as to effect the most widespread utilization of the human potential. The opinion expressed on this subject by Arthur Lewis,[1] André Philip[2] and Bertrand de Jouvenel[3] would seem to be entirely justified : "The method which would be the most economical where capital is relatively abundant compared with labour is wasteful where capital is rather scarce in comparison with labour."[4]

The Need for Planning

An examination of the choice between social or economic equipment, and between agriculture or industry, leads to two discoveries. On the one hand, development implies a balanced effort made in several fields, and on the other hand the precise details of this equilibrium vary from case to case. This organic unity of national development, together with national variations in the conditions for growth, suggest that each backward country requires a separate synthesis of intelligence and will in which the required combination may be perceived and carried through.

---

[1] The Theory of Economic Growth, pp. 385-7.
[2] Europe and the Underdeveloped Countries, Report to the European Labour Congress, Nouvelles de l'Europe (International Bulletin of the European Movement) August—September 1956, p. 9.
[3] op. cit. pp. 25-28.
[4] Jouvenel, op. cit. p. 26. These considerations to some extent justify Gandhi's preference for "Cottage industries", which one might be tempted at first to put down to a rather medieval spiritual outlook.

Governments alone are in a position to fulfil this task, whether or not their efforts are seconded by private initiative.

The cardinal role of government in development is confirmed by the recent history of countries which have triumphed over their backwardness, whether we think of Communist countries or of non-Communist ones such as Australia or Japan. It may be objected that this is not how growth took place in Western Europe and North America. It is indeed true that the development of the West happened in a much more liberal way (though we have to guard against the habit, dear to Western people, of over-estimating the role of private initiative in past centuries. A close examination reveals far more state intervention and royal manu-facturers than is usually thought to have existed). But the con-ditions of growth have meanwhile changed radically. The devel-opment of the West was favoured alike by the climate, by the current philosophy (Christianity, especially in its Protestant form, encourages individual effort in the temporal sphere, unlike many religions whose outlook is both more collective and less interested in this world), and perhaps also by race. For although the West has exaggerated this idea outrageously, it is possible that biologi-cal factors make the European, not indeed better in every way, but better adapted to the requirements of economic progress.[1] And, above all, during their growth period the European coun-tries had two trump cards which the underdeveloped countries of today do not possess, namely space and time.

Space : A country which was developing two centuries ago could draw upon all the rest of the world, finding suppliers of raw material and consumers for its finished products. Indeed, Great Britain drew a large part of the capital for its industrial expansion from trade with less developed countries. World space was mobilized in the service of the developing nation. Today, on the other hand, a country wishing to develop itself is surrounded by a shoal of competitors well equipped in apparatus and ex-

[1] It should not however be forgotten that the population of a large part of the Indian continent and of the Middle East is probably closely related to the predominant races of Europe.

perience and quite ready, if need be, to demand from their Governments, when they see their outlets imperilled, protection for their home market or assistance for their exports.

The West had time too : it took several centuries to emerge from what is nowadays known as underdevelopment. It was a very long time before agricultural surplus enabled industrial investment to be made. Such leisurely growth towards maturity is no longer possible; underdeveloped countries are compelled to go more quickly : the sight of the developed ones makes them impatient and furthermore, to compete in world markets they must begin with the high standards of quality which the same industry has attained in countries whose development is of long standing. The whole complex production must be assimilated at one go, and this leap as regards quality often necessitates a leap as regards quantity as well. For instance, it would not be reasonable nowadays to think of a steelworks producing less than a million tons a year. Backward countries are denied that progressive development which would make the task of adaptation so much easier.

Sometimes, of course, the natural conditions are such as to facilitate this leap; two examples of this were mentioned earlier.[1] Nevertheless, the planning role of the government remains fundamental even in such cases. The sudden irruption, without any intermediate stage, of vast modern organizations into a primitive world threatens to cause serious damage to the economic and social fabric. It is a complex task, and one which cannot be left to chance, to see that this new body is properly introduced into the social organism.

But circumstances are not usually so favourable to these big leaps. And this leads governments to assume even greater responsibilities. They sometimes have to make good the lack of business leaders and act in their stead. There may be nationals or foreigners who could run businesses, but who will not do so because they are afraid of the primitive economic surroundings. Suitable business men, when approached, refuse because they are

[1] cf. Chapter X, p. 113.

afraid the country will not contain enough other industrialists to provide either a market or sources of supply or a pool of labour. Industry attracts more industry; development attracts further development. Conversely, a state of underdevelopment tends to perpetuate itself. The only philosophy which can break this vicious circle is that of an organic development in which each undertaking helps to underpin the others.

There are other aspects to this problem of the economic environment. In an underdeveloped country, lack of basic public services such as power production, roads or tools for the labour force, hinders or prevents the establishment of business enterprises and, unusually favourable cases excepted, governments are compelled to assume responsibility for providing these facilities.

One last remark about the economic environment. In the West the capital goods industries grew up simultaneously with the processing industries, and the relative simplicity of the techniques then in use made this much easier. Today, however, a country which is becoming industrialized usually has to import its capital equipment, and this raises balance of payments problems serious enough to warrant a fairly strict control of foreign trade. This is one more reason why governmental action in such circumstances is essential.

Thus economic growth appears inevitably to involve planning activity by the state. It is this activity which replaces the benefits which the first countries to be industrialized obtained naturally because they were blessed with both time and space in sufficient quantity.

Chapter Twelve

INTELLECTUAL AID

SINCE GOVERNMENT planning should be carried out with the most up-to-date knowledge and methods, intellectual aid from the developed nations is desirable.

The expression "intellectual aid" is used in preference to the more usual ones of "technical assistance" and "technical co-operation" because the words "assistance", "co-operation", and "technical" do not fully convey the required meaning. The word "assistance" is considered offensive. The use of the word "co-operation" is only a euphemism invented to replace "assistance", though it has the advantage of suggesting that the nation receiving the assistance ought to take some positive action as well as the nation giving it.[1]

As for the word "technical", it should be understood in its widest meaning, as contrasted with the word "financial". Thus the gift of capital is a form of financial assistance, whilst grey matter is technical assistance. But still it is not the best word, because the meaning just suggested is not that which is usually given to it; it is a narrower meaning having to do with the handling of material things, whereas assistance concerned with material techniques, whether industrial, agricultural or other, is only one aspect of what is rightly called technical assistance, which does

[1] See below, p. 146.

not consist only in showing poor countries how to build a bridge or a factory, but also how to evolve a plan or to set up a system of taxation or an administration. For this reason, the expression "intellectual aid" is preferred because "aid" is a more neutral word than "assistance" or "co-operation" and "intellectual" has a wider meaning than "technical".

Intellectual aid today

Private intellectual aid came first in order of time. For many years initiatives inspired by religion or humanitarianism have occupied an important place in aid to underdeveloped countries. Indeed, in the last few decades, the economic expansion of America has given a new impetus to this kind of assistance, as witness the vast projects undertaken by the Rockefeller Foundation, the Ford Foundation, the Carnegie Foundation and similar institutions.

Apart from disinterested activity of this kind, private intellectual aid is more or less directly motivated by the search for profits which, however, can be carried on in one of two ways. It can be given freely as an indirect way of promoting the success of a financial investment or of some commercial expansion, or it may be paid for, the object then being the direct sale of grey matter at a profit.

The traditional method is the first one. For an undertaking to prosper in an underdeveloped country it must put down certain roots into the local economy. The investor tries to make the inhabitants of the country into users of his product or suppliers of the raw materials necessary for it, or to become useful workers in his business. For example, a business the object of which is to transform local products will often find it a good idea to give technical assistance towards improving the quality or the quantity of the products in question.

Even if the factory is not situated in the underdeveloped country, action of this sort on the local economy can still be well worthwhile. In that case intellectual aid is serving commercial expansion rather than financial investment. A good example of this are the excellent courses in elementary mechanics which manufacturers of tractors or agricultural machines have given in underdeveloped countries.

Intellectual aid for which a fee is charged has developed much more recently. Consultants' offices have been set up or, if they were already in existence, have adapted themselves to the task of giving technical assistance in underdeveloped countries. Their only object is to do work for which they are paid, either from the budgets of the underdeveloped countries themselves, or from grants which these governments receive from various foreign or international organizations.[1]

Most intellectual aid nowadays is given in the public sector under bi-lateral or multi-lateral arrangements.

The oldest form of bi-lateral aid, and one of the most important, is that which is given by some industrialized countries, especially Great Britain and France, but also Belgium, Holland, Spain and Portugal, to underdeveloped countries which have special political and economic ties with them.

In dependent territories, the metropolitan states send administrators part of whose task is to maintain order or to exercise authority, but who in many cases include specialists in various techniques, some material and some non-material, which foster either directly or indirectly, the country's growth; examples are geologists, hydrologists, statisticians etc.[2] Sometimes these administrators are paid by the home country, but it is more usual for their salaries to be paid from the local budget; yet even where

[1] There is not always a very clear distinction between these two forms of private aid. There may be consultants' offices having close connections with industrial groups which supply the material or the product in question, or with public works organizations who are interested in the work arising from such schemes. Consultants' offices of this type receive payment, but they have a complex objective and are partly engaged in an attempt to attract orders. This means that an office of this type may sometimes function at a loss since its aim is, at least in part, extrinsic to itself. In extreme cases its activity is a clever form of market research on the part of the group to which it belongs.

[2] It would also be a mistake to think that it is only these various technical specialists who place their knowledge at the service of the country's development. French administrators in overseas territories, for instance, whether central or local, are traditionally jacks-of-all-trades, who besides exercising authority look after roads, canals, co-operatives, provident societies, etc.

this is so the home country is still giving something, because she has had the prior expense of educating them and she also has a contingent expense arising from the guarantee of continuity for their careers, whether this is formal or purely a moral guarantee.[1]

Though the posting of officials at the discretion of the home country is becoming increasingly outmoded, metropolitan aid survives vigorously in the form of placing a certain number of executives at the disposal of a state or of an autonomous territory. Even in newly independent states, wherever separation from the former ruling country has been carried through without a psychological and political break, a large number of officials who are nationals of the former ruling country still remain at work.

Even so, this formula may be unwelcome in countries where a sensitive nationalism reigns. This has given rise to a new formula whereby the ruling country or the former ruling country finances intellectual aid which is administered by public or semi-public organizations. Usually this form of aid is financed from the investment credits opened by the metropolitan or ex-metropolitan country in favour of the dependent or formerly dependent territories. For example, in the french-speaking African countries a considerable portion of the credits granted by the FAC is allocated to intellectual investments,[2] and the same thing applies within the various groups in different parts of the world

[1] In the African countries belonging to the French Community a third constant expense is added to the initial and the contingent ones. It consists of certain payments made from the home budget over and above the basic salary which is paid by the local government.

[2] The FIDES works principally through public organizations such as research institutes dedicated to each of the main tropical products, the Office for Overseas Scientific and Technical Research, the Bureau of Geological and Mining Research, the Central Planning Office for Overseas Equipment, the Bureau for the Development of Overseas Agricultural Production, the French Company for the Development of Textile Fibres, and the General Company for Tropical Oil Products. In addition, specialists employed by the State though not in organizations of this type, are often called upon to carry out particular studies, as are also public companies not set up for operation overseas, such as the Electricité de France, or private companies, as for instance, Ugine, and Pierrefitte which were called in for the Kouilou project in Central Congo. A fair estimate of the expenses for technical assistance of this type throughout the former "overseas territories" would be about 25 million dollars a year. If North Africa and the overseas "Départements" are added, the total would doubtless be in the region of 50 million dollars a year.

which include in their membership both developed and under-developed countries.[1]

More recently, bilateral intellectual assistance agreements between countries not having special political or economic ties have in turn developed considerably.

For upwards of fifteen years, the United States have been operating a technical assistance programme administered in the main under the International Co-operation Administration, although certain parts of it come directly under the control of the State Department or belong to the Atomic Energy Commission. This programme has many facets: Agriculture, industry, transport, housing, health, education, trades unions and administration. The methods it uses are very varied. It sends out technicians,[2] trains specialists from the underdeveloped countries[3] in the United States or in third countries,[4] sets up teaching institutions in the underdeveloped countries themselves, in co-operation with American Universities[5] and distributes written, photographic or cinematographic material and visual aids. Every year the United States devote about 200 million dollars to technical assistance, including not only bilateral action but also that undertaken through the United Nations and the Organization of American States.

[1] As regards Great Britain, dependent territories receive technical assistance financed by part of the "Colonial Development and Welfare Acts" Funds. It can be estimated that 10 million dollars a year are allocated to technical assistance out of an overall total of 40 to 50 million dollars a year. On the other hand, Great Britain gives nothing but technical assistance to the countries of the Colombo Plan, either by sending out 50 to 100 experts each year or by receiving students and learners, of whom between 125 and 250 come annually. But thirdly, Great Britain undoubtedly gives technical assistance to the other sterling area countries to the value of several hundred million dollars.

[2] There are about seven thousand American specialists in underdeveloped countries.

[3] About ten thousand are undergoing courses of instruction wholly financed by bursaries from America.

[4] The American Government likes to use American institutions situated in third countries, such as the American University in Beirut, the Technical Co-operation Laboratory in Porto Rico, or the International Institute of Agricultural Science at Turrialba in Costa Rica. For Asia and the Pacific Ocean countries, the Hawaiian Islands and Japan are often used as relay stations.

[5] At the end of 1956 80 contracts of this type had been signed, associating 54 universities in the United States with projects in 38 overseas countries.

Other non-Communist countries do much less in this sphere. Canada sends a few dozen experts abroad and receives a few hundred students and trainees, mainly under the Colombo Plan. Great Britain's activity is difficult to measure because it is dispersed over a number of organizations such as the British Council, the British Middle East Development Division, the Bagdad Pact, etc. But the total does not appear to be very large since Britain, on the other hand, makes very great use of multilateral procedures.

In France the greater part of this type of activity is sponsored jointly by the Ministry of Foreign Affairs and the Ministry of Economic Affairs, and between two and three million dollars a year have been given to it during the last few years. This amounts to the sending out of nearly 500 experts and the reception of more than 1,500 students and people on vocational courses.

The amount of technical assistance given by Germany has increased rapidly during the last few years. Since the credits devoted to this work recently have not been in the form of annual payments, it is difficult to say exactly how they compare from year to year; but there is little doubt that the credits given by Germany amount to many times the value of the French credits and still more of those given by Britain—though this remark excludes the considerable effort made by each of these countries in the territories belonging to their respective currency areas.

Countries such as Sweden and Norway also carry out quite sizeable programmes.

During the last few years the USSR and its allies, too, have been responsible for quite a costly programme. In December 1960 there were more than 8,000 technicians from Soviet Russia in non-communist underdeveloped countries, though many of them were sent only for very short periods. Moreover, nearly 12,000 students from underdeveloped countries have attended courses in civil or military teaching establishments in the Communist *bloc* during the last six years.

The United Nations and its specialized organizations are the main channel for intellectual aid which is given multi-laterally. Only a very small part of the necessary funds come from the specialized institutions, most of the money is supplied by the UNO itself and its credits have been considerably stepped up on two occasions for this purpose, mainly in 1950[1] and in 1957.[2] It now has a budget of about one hundred million dollars a year. According to the purpose for which these funds are to be used, they are administered by the appropriate specialized organizations of the United Nations (mainly the FAO, UNESCO, the World Health Organizations and the International Labour Office), as well as by the Technical Assistance Administration, which emanates directly from the general secretariat of the United Nations. The latter deals with matters which are not within the province of any of the specialized organizations and the whole is co-ordinated by the Technical Assistance Board which centralizes requests and tries to secure uniformity of methods.

Up till 1957 action by the United Nations took the form mainly of seconding experts (between 2,000 and 3,000 going each year to underdeveloped countries), and of giving scholarships for the completion of studies (rather more than 2,000 a year going to underdeveloped countries).

Thanks to the much larger resources now at its disposal the United Nations Administration plans, in addition, to finance the study of some special projects touching on various basic problems, such as research on hydrological resources as well as resources of minerals and power, the establishment of colleges for public administration, statistics and technology, the supply of personnel and equipment for them, and the financing of research and productivity centres for agriculture and industry.

[1] In 1950 an enlarged programme additional to the previous one was launched, known as the EPTANU (Enlarged Programme of Technical Assistance of the United Nations).

[2] In 1958 the plan for a large fund to be known as SUNFED (Special United Nations Fund for Economic Development) which would have been used to finance investment in underdeveloped countries was shelved—finally, as it seems—largely owing to opposition from the United States. At the same time as a consolation prize, a special fund for technical and social assistance to underdeveloped countries was established with the object of reinforcing the UN's technical assistance programme. Its budget amounted to 24 million dollars in 1959 and 45 million dollars in 1960.

UNO assists only governments, not private enterprises. It usually asks for a financial contribution from the country concerned, especially for the costs of lodging, travel and the supply of offices and secretarial staff. Where the size of the tasks in view seems to justify it the Technical Assistance Board stations a permanent representative in the underdeveloped country, especially when the latter appears to find difficulty in formulating its own requests for intellectual aid.

The United States is by far the largest contributor to this programme. With regard to the utilization of these credits, it is interesting to note that the United States receives somewhat fewer scholarship holders than Great Britain, and a little more than France; the situation is the same as far as the number of experts is concerned.

One activity of the United Nations, a form of intellectual aid which is as yet quite minor, but which could become very large, is worthy of mention. This is the International Civil Service, consisting of officials placed at the disposal of underdeveloped countries, not to carry out a particular task, but to form an integral part of their own administrative organization where such countries do not themselves have enough competent persons to carry out certain responsibilities. At present only about fifteen such officials are at work, seconded to Nepal, Sudan, Libya, Panama, Malaya, Burma, Laos, Tunisia and Jamaica; half their remuneration is paid by the UNO and half by the country employing them. It may also be noted that at present they are acting as advisers rather than in a management capacity.

The activity of the Regional Economic Commissions of UNO, consists in carrying out studies of a general nature which may help the countries in question to gain a clear appreciation of their own problems. One of them, the ECAFE,[1] is giving actual technical assistance on its own account independently of the UNO programme itself, but this is unique so far.

The International Bank, too, gives advice to countries requesting it, on problems of harnessing their resources, even if the ques-

[1] The Economic Commission for Asia and the Far East.

tions asked do not have a direct connection with requests for loans. Up to the beginning of 1960, nineteen missions had been sent out by the International Bank to various member countries to study their resources and their economic potential or to help them with planning. Missions are also sent to study particular development problems. The bánk has permanent representatives in certain countries who are available as advisers. It has also set up an Economic Development Institute, which organizes study course lasting six months for officials (or even politicians) from underdeveloped countries.

Principles of Action

It is clear from the above survey that the industrialized nations are making considerable efforts as regards intellectual aid, so much so that if the whole of this effort were directed and placed with perfect accuracy, it might well be sufficient for the needs of the underdeveloped countries. But intellectual aid depends for its full efficiency on the fulfilment of various conditions; it must be a dialogue, and it must go hand in hand with financial assistance.

It has to be a dialogue because the idea of a backward country receiving intellectual aid quite passively and with no attempt to take part in the creative process is almost a contradiction in terms. The object is always to evolve a plan or a taxation system or technical improvements which, though they may be the brain children of foreigners, are capable of being applied and used by the country itself. Technical assistance which does not have the character of a dialogue is like the help which, through laziness or incompetence, parents sometimes give to their children when they do their homework for them instead of showing them how to do it. The most effective intellectual aid always has a pedagogic aspect. This aspect is obvious when the intellectual aid takes the form of receiving students from the underdeveloped country, but it is still there, even though less obvious, when the intellectual aid consists of sending experts to the country. For there should be such a collaboration between the experts and the nationals of the country that in the end, as in the old trade guilds, fully trained apprentices able to work on their own will be turned out. The aim is not merely to supply some grey matter, but to place the underdeveloped country in a position to exploit its own reserves of grey matter, both now and, even more importantly, later on.

It follows from this conception of intellectual aid as a dialogue, that helper and helped must know one another sufficiently well to speak the same language; and this, first of all, in the most literal meaning of the expression. If intellectual aid consisted in publishing a learned treatise on a given subject, the expert could write it in his own language and have it translated afterwards; but in technical assistance, the work of the expert involves a constant intercourse with the local people. Moreover, language is only the outward vehicle for an essential minimum of common ideas between teacher and taught. It is obvious that not every developed country, even armed with knowledge and goodwill, has the vocation of giving intellectual aid immediately to every underdeveloped country.

Of course this minimum of common understanding is not something which is predetermined. It can be acquired provided that the developed country in question is willing to specialize, which the Scandinavian countries, for example, have very wisely done. Instead of trying to spread themselves over the entire world, they have selected certain spheres of work in which they have gradually acquired a very real competence.

Clearly, however, linguistic affiliations, which are usually linked in some degree with geographical proximity and with historical connections of long standing, furnish some ready-made patterns of which advantage should be taken.

For example, an industrial country which during the colonial period had special links with an underdeveloped one, in which therefore knowledge of its language and of its way of thinking is fairly widespread, has a special responsibility to preserve such links by transmuting them into intellectual aid—unless through misfortune or its own mishandling of the situation this becomes impossible for political reasons.

Intellectual aid must also go hand in hand with financial assistance. In theory, no doubt, the two are separate. Financial assistance can be given without intellectual aid if its purpose is to carry out a programme which has been planned by the indigenous authority.

Conversely, intellectual aid without financial assistance can be imagined, for example if the work of technical advisers is paid for, as happens with consultants' offices; though even then the payment should cover the total cost of such specialists, including that of their education and the assurance of their future.

It is desirable for psychological reasons to keep the administration of intellectual aid separate from that of financial assistance. To a susceptible nation, intellectual and financial responsibility held jointly could create an unpleasant impression of high-handedness. It does not therefore seem desirable to have in the developed countries organizations which carry both these responsibilities at once.

Yet it is indispensable for the two forms of aid to be closely linked and properly co-ordinated. Financial aid without technical assistance is apt to lead to waste. The risks of degeneracy attaching to foreign aid were mentioned in Chapter XI.[1] One of the surest ways of avoiding such deterioration is to allocate part of the financial aid to financing the intellectual aid which is needed for the proper planning and execution of investment projects. If financial aid calls for intellectual aid, the reverse is also true. For one thing, intellectual aid is very often given without payment. But that is not enough. Financial aid should not only cover the intellectual aid, it should also prolong it and enable it to carry out its own advice. Too often today the underdeveloped countries receive technical assistance in generous measure, but hardly any money to buy equipment. It is as though the Health Service were offering a dying man consultations with the most famous doctors without giving him the money to buy a bottle of aspirin, and were letting him die of fever whilst his bedside table was piled high with magnificent prescriptions.

[1] pp. 100-101.

In the last resort intellectual aid without financial assistance is only a sophism, as though to say : "I have told you free of charge what to do, and there my responsibility ends."

This of course, does not escape the most honest amongst those who are administering intellectual aid. An attempt was made in the United Nations to overcome it, and the great project of SUNFED[1] was discussed, but instead of the thousands of millions of dollars which would have been necessary, it was only possible to collect a few tens of millions. What could be done with this? Spread over the whole world it was sufficient only for technical assistance, and that is what was done with it.

The result is that, for the moment, of all the possible objects of financial aid, free technical assistance is the only one which is properly covered; in some respects indeed it is over-endowed; better co-ordination would enable some economies to be made. But it cannot bear its real fruit until the investment which is known to be necessary can be financed partly by national savings and partly by aid from abroad. From this point of view, the remarkable spurt which intellectual aid has shown in the last ten years, and the present state of effort in the world, constitute a useful start—but only a start.

It is also worth noting that the way in which the various developed nations jointly contribute technical assistance, could well serve as a model for financial assistance. In the first place, a large part of this assistance is given through multilateral organizations; and we have seen that it would be desirable for financial assistance to develop along multilateral lines.[2]

Then, even under the form of bilateral assistance there is a fairer division of effort between the various industrialized nations than there is in regard to public investment in the underdeveloped countries. The United States are the leaders in both cases, but their lead in intellectual aid is much larger than in investment; a logical division of effort is more closely approached. The distribution of intellectual aid among the various receiving coun-

[1] Compare above, p. 144. Note 2.
[2] Compare Chapter IX, p. 100.

tries is also more satisfactory than that of financial aid; there are
not the same anomalies.[1]

The considerable programme of technical assistance now going
on throughout the world, which by itself is liable to remain ster-
ile, will become really fruitful if the rich nations learn how to
graft financial assistance on to intellectual aid before it is too late.

[1] Compare Chapter IX, pp. 100-101 and XVI, p. 184.

Chapter Thirteen

PSYCHOLOGICAL AND POLITICAL CONDITIONS

WE HAVE seen that development calls both for knowledge of the nation's assets and the will to put them to work and transform them. In other words, it involves an intellectual act and an act of will. In theory the intellectual act can be brought in from outside through technical assistance, though, as we have just seen, even this presupposes for full efficiency mutual understanding with the nationals of the country to be assisted. But in any event nobody can will the nation's growth in substitution for the nation itself. On what conditions can this will exist? We are speaking of will, not just of a passing desire.

There appear to be two basic conditions—the re-conversion of social structures and ideals, and the creation of a strong government.

Development demands faith in development; *a nation cannot grow without believing in growth.* Now, in many underdeveloped countries a certain lack of interest in the values of a social economy of modern type is observable. In general such societies are not orientated towards material progress, increasing wellbeing and mastery over nature.[1]

[1] See especially Georges Balandier, Le Contexte Socio-culturel et le Coût Social du Progrès, pp. 289-303 of the symposium *Le Tiers Monde.*

151

Thus, in the Sudan region of Africa horned cattle are a sign of riches and not a source of riches, because they are not exploited in any way. In India, transmuted by their sacred character, they even become a source of poverty. In certain societies in Central and South America competition is forbidden; to be more successful than other members of society is not done. The right use for wealth is often thought to be prestige expenditure, conspicuous waste or land speculation rather than productive employment. In many backward countries there is a more or less rigid ban on the possession of any personal income; this is quite categorical among the Indians of Bolivia, which leads modern-minded individuals among them to leave the country. It is more or less latent in Black Africa where the whole family, in the most grotesquely wide meaning of the word, descends upon any of its members who has acquired some gain to share it with him.

Obviously, in such cases there must be a change in structures and ideals before development can take place. As the American economic historian Gerschenkron put it, there must be "an emotional new deal."[1]

Whenever a leap forward has occurred in history, it has always been associated with such an "emotional new deal". The beginnings of Communism in the USSR were accompanied by such a phenomenon. Earlier on, the Japanese metamorphosis of 1875 was bound up with a religious reaction among the Samurai in which Shintoism was restored and the cult of the Emperor re-affirmed against Buddhism from China.

Earlier still, there have been at least two capitalist impulses in the West which did not result in accelerated growth. In the 13th century the capital accumulated by the merchants did not increase the pace of development because, absorbed in the traditional interests of their age, they used it only to acquire land. Again in the sixteenth century there was a renewed surge of mercantile capitalist activity; but its fruits were used largely to finance the Renaissance which, from the economic point of view, was an immense and unforgettable effusion of sumptuary expenditure. The industrial revolution was born two centuries later in Great Britain

[1] Quoted by G. Balandier, op. cit. p. 293.

when, in addition to a number of other favourable factors, a religious movement among the middle classes convinced its adherents that to attain salvation it was necessary to produce much but consume little, luxury being sinful and gain a mark of election.

It can hardly be expected that backward countries will draw their emotional new deal from the springs of some such neo-puritanism. Nonetheless, the will to achieve national development really needs the support of an appropriate psychological stimulus. Where then should those nations seek the necessary emotional drive?

It is wise to begin with existing realities and seek to adapt them to the requirements of a modern outlook. For example, efforts are being made in India to base development on the village communities and indeed to give the traditional village assemblies a voice in the development planning itself. For, generally speaking, the peasant's instinctive and almost biological attachment to the soil contains the germ of a will to development which can be made explicit and conscious by an agrarian reform giving legal status and the guarantee of permanance to these ties.

But besides these ancient loyalties, all available modern channels of inspiration should be pressed into service. Very often a political party may be the appropriate medium, as it is in Ghana and in some of the countries of the French Community.

Finally, any idea which may awaken a response from public opinion as a whole, or a large section of it, should be enlisted in support of this will to growth. The nationalist sentiment now so widespread among backward nations can, for instance, be harnessed to this end. It can, indeed, canalize such national aspirations into wholesome paths and away from the crude desire for conquest.

This, no doubt, is the road a Nehru would wish to take—even though he has not so far avoided nationalistic attitudes over Kashmir, to say nothing of Goa. Nasser's Egypt too, it would seem, now finds itself at the parting of the ways between two conceptions of the nations. There is the country's own consciousness of its nationhood leading it to concentrate all its energy on growth; Arab nationalism, on the other hand, would tempt it to spend all its energies for *accretion*. Clearly nationalism is an idea which can be harnessed either to development or to struggle and impoverishment.

These considerations take us to the heart of the political problems of development.

No country in course of development can do without a strong government, for it needs compulsion and enthusiasm within and confidence abroad.

Compulsion is needed to overcome obstacles to growth, whether feudal land tenure, parasitic middle men or even, from some points of view, an excessive birth rate (for the introduction of birth control is bound to do violence to the social conscience). Similarly, compulsion is needed to stimulate investment, whether by mopping up excess incomes, or by actualizing potential savings through putting surplus labour to work on national projects. Moreover, investment must be devoted to productive enterprises —not as in the Philippines, where observers noted with some astonishment that it had been lavished mainly on equipping cinemas.

Still, the sacrifices called for by development cannot all be forcibly imposed. There must be a civic consciousness willing to accept them as necessary. To give up psychosociological attitudes inimical to progress, the people must become imbued with the Government's own ideals. Government must rest on the people's active acquiescence, but it must also know how to win that allegiance.

Lastly, foreign aid, whether public or private, will not be attracted unless the image which the underdeveloped country presents to the outside world has certain qualities which inspire confidence. Contrary to the opinion of some superficial observers, the quality most apt to inspire confidence is not pliability but strength. For only such strength can make the other party feel that the agreement extends spatially beyond the government to the nation as a whole, and that consequently it is secure in time also, since government by consent confers security of office on those who made the agreement, and even their going would not necessarily endanger it.

The existence of a strong government without which development can scarcely take place, itself raises certain implications.

The first of these is self-determination. No government can enjoy the authority needed to stimulate development in its country unless it is regarded by the people both as validly representing them and also as possessing sufficient responsibility in the exercise of its powers.

This problem particularly affects countries which, because they are or were overseas possessions, have special political and economic links with industrialized ones. The attitude of mind too often prevalent in such countries, which is to importune the metropolis for solutions to their problems, strikes at the root of healthy, responsible development. Governments of under-developed countries must consciously assume their responsibilities for the nation's evolution. One of the key activities of the legistla-ture and the executive in doing this will be to draw up their own plan of development. This does not mean as many are tempted to believe, devizing schemes for spending money given by the metropolis. It means first finding at home, through effort and sacrifice, the means of fulfilling the plan, though parts of it may be carried out with financial help from the metropolitan country, under varying contractual agreements considered by both parties to be advantageous.

This sense of self-determination can of course operate within the framework of a larger community of which the backward country is a member. But this implies that where decisions of the larger community impinge upon the country, they must appear as agreed measures, not as external demands.

Moreover let it not be thought that present or former "over-seas territories" are alone in having problems of self-determina-tion. The South American States gained their independence more than a century ago, yet they feel themselves, not without apparent justification, to be dependent upon a power whose Vice-President was lately the object of hostile behaviour in their streets. In other words, self-determination implies more than formal political independence, it includes also the feeling that the economic life of the country is not wholly dependent upon a foreign nation. (It is suggestive that in his *Conversations with Nehru*[1] Monsieur Tibor Mende proposed the use of the term "Latin-Americanization" for this new type of satellite relationship.)

Whether a country ceased to be a colony only recently or a long time ago, its growth demands so much emotional drive that the government is compelled to use every opportunity of generating it. Balandier[2] writes: "The need to win public support for modernization and the introduction of industrial civilization leads the responsible leaders in underdeveloped countries to harness the strength of the hostility which the people feel towards the nations who created this very civilization, who were the first to feel its benefits, and who for long monopolized and abused its privileges."

This use of the capacity of primitive peoples for nationalism and zenophobia can of course be a bitter pill for the nations "who created this industrial civilization" especially if, rightly or wrongly, they feel that, all things considered, they did not in fact "abuse its privileges."

Such nations may indeed have other and still more potent reasons for bitterness. Suffice it to mention here one implication—a very delicate one—of the installation of strong governments.

Seen from afar, a strong government conveys an idea of reassuring stability. But it must be said in all honesty that a closer view, in backward countries, almost inevitably reveals meddling by the executives with the judicial function, loss of guarantees for the opposition, rigged elections, single-party rule or an approximation thereto—in a word a flirtation with totalitarianism. Frenchmen who welcomed the development of Black Africa since the outline law of 1956 now see the strong governments which have come to power in certain French possessions or former possessions repudiating the rules of the democratic system which

[1] cf. especially p. 128.
[2] op. cit. p. 294.

they would like to have seen accepted. But perhaps this is just the last expression of the principle of assimilation[1]—the lingering desire to have a say in the internal management of a country where they have ceased to rule. It must surely be accepted that the nations belonging to the French Community will not all choose the same system of government. France's Cartesianism must needs make this last sacrifice.

We must frankly face the fact that the democratic forms dear to the West are almost non-existent in underdeveloped countries, and there is much truth in Monsieur Tibor Mende's opinion that there are only two kinds of régimes in poor countries—authoritarian governments seeking to perpetuate existing inequalities and authoritarian governments working for reform.

[1] Whereas the British adopt a more paternalistic attitude to their dependencies, the French practice, following the Roman system, is to offer the full benefits of French culture and citizenship (extending even to representation in the metropolitan legislature) to all their subjects who desire and qualify for them.

Part III

THE POLITICS AND GEOPOLITICS OF DEVELOPMENT

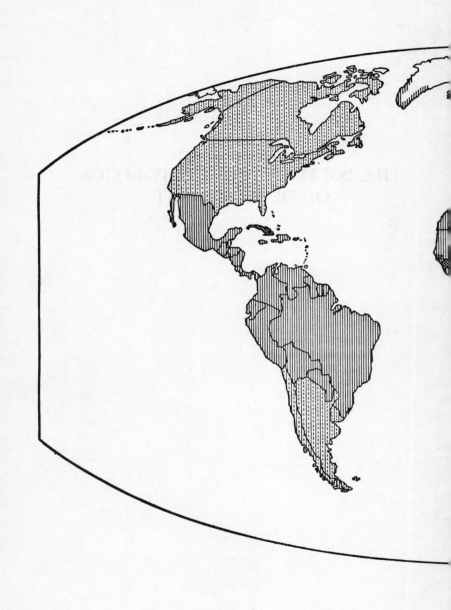

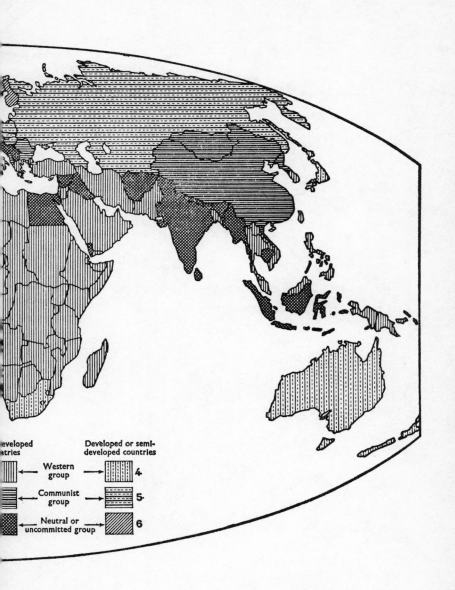

eveloped atries	Developed or semi-developed countries	
Western group		4
Communist group		5
Neutral or uncommitted group		6

Chapter Fourteen

THE POLITICAL STAKES

THE UNDERDEVELOPED countries may be classified in three groups more or less equal in size, as shown on the map.

Broadly speaking, Latin America (except Cuba), the Countries of Southern Europe, Africa excluding Egypt and Guinea and a discontinuous band of Asian states, with a total population of more than 600 million, make up the group friendly to the West. At the other extreme come China with some adjacent countries, and various underdeveloped countries in Eastern Europe, members of the Communist *bloc,* their populations totalling about 680 millions. Between these two is a group of Asian countries (of which India is the most important) and Middle Eastern ones (of which the United Arab Republic is the most important) who, together with Yugoslavia, Guinea and Cuba form a neutral or neutralist group having a total population of a little less than 600 million.

There are also developed or semi-developed countries corresponding to each of these groups, having chosen the same political attitude. Those corresponding to the first group form the West, and include North America, most of Western Europe, Australia and New Zealand (the most highly developed ones in the world) and also South Africa, the Southern part of South America, and Japan, totalling some 600 million people of whom about 400 million live in highly developed countries. The USSR and the industrialized countries of Eastern Europe, with 250 million people belong to the second group. The third group, neutral or neutralist, also has opposite numbers in various stages of development, Finland, Sweden, Switzerland, Austria and Ireland, containing some 25 million people.

But the neutral or neutralist group does not look to the last named countries for massive support. On the contrary, it clearly leans heavily on the other two groups of industrial states, playing them off against one another. Nor is this third group the only theatre of rivalry between the other two, for the frontier between all three groups is a shifting one. States have changed their allegiance in the more or less recent past—Yugoslavia in one direction and various states in the Middle East and South East Asia in the other one.

The two main political groups watch this frontier closely; and whilst the third group is the only one to receive aid from both sides, the underdeveloped countries in the Communist group sometimes receive offers from the West, and conversely Russia often makes approaches to underdeveloped countries in the Western camp. These subversive offers, or even the possibility of their being made, make their more powerful allies so uneasy that they in turn try to do more as a counter-attraction. Thus each ideological camp finds in the existence of the other one a compelling reason for helping underdeveloped countries.

There are both political and economic reasons for the passionate determination of the developed countries to maintain or increase their influence among the underprivileged ones, and they are dealt with in that order in this chapter and the next.

The possibility of war is always implicit in the competition between the two camps. Thus the first aspect from which the struggle for the underdeveloped countries should be seen is the strategic one. For each has a strategic advantage of some kind, as potential suppliers of some of the sinews of war to one side or the other, or at least a manoeuvring space for them.

The sinews of war are raw materials and men; we shall return to the former in Chapter XV. As for men, the inhabitants of an underdeveloped country can be used as soldiers by the alliance to which their country belongs. It is indeed quite accepted in the United States that a soldier who is a native of an underdeveloped country costs far less than an American soldier. The presence in the Soviet camp of China, that reservoir of humanity, enables the Communists to adopt a strategy of overwhelming their opponents by sheer numbers.[1]

It may be said that nuclear weapons are lessening the importance of infantry; but, apart from the fact that nuclear war may not come, belligerent nations are bound to make plans for occupying the territory, however it is conquered.

It is the spatial aspects of strategic ideas which are of much more concern to underdeveloped countries for they may be situated close to a vital centre belonging to one side or the other, or control a communication route either wholly or partly, or constitute territory useful for deployment or other purposes.

Certainly proximity is becoming less important, and the idea of strategic bases is becoming less and less essential, for the effective range of modern weapons and techniques of flight refuelling place all parts of the earth within striking distance of all other parts. The whole world is becoming a single theatre of operations.

Now that ICBM's (inter-continental ballistic missiles) have reached a high degree of precision and have been manufactured in large numbers by both camps, the idea of strategic bases can legitimately be described as *technically* out of date. Yet it is a fact of experience that nations may hesitate to use certain crushing weapons they possess, either because of scruples or from fear of reprisals. Wars therefore could still be fought at a lower technical level than what is theoretically available. Consequently, the idea of strategic bases has not lost its practical importance, and this means that the Great Powers may still wish to have under-

---

[1] In 1943 the USSR could field 600 divisions; in theory the USSR and China could now field 2,400 divisions jointly, (ignoring the question of arming and supplying them).

developed countries as friends or allies, either to facilitate their own plans for attack or to deny the potential adversary a like advantage.

This is why both the United States and her potential enemies are interested in Latin America. The Pacific region is of interest to the United States, and supremely so to Australia and New Zealand, and also to their potential enemies. The countries of Western Europe, and their potential enemies, are interested in Mediterranean Africa, Eastern Europe and to a smaller degree tropical Africa. In the three cases just cited, if we except Eastern Europe and part of the near East, the underdeveloped countries in question are in general allies of the Western cause, though with varying degrees of commitment and enthusiasm. But only some of the backward states surrounding the USSR are controlled by or allied to the USSR. Her southern marches border on many countries which are either neutral or allied to the West. This is even more true of Russia and China considered as a *bloc*. For this *bloc* is enclosed not only on the South but also on the East by countries most of which are backward, and most of which are either neutral of allies of the West.

It is true that the vast continental spaces of the Russo-Chinese mass are in themselves a protection. And the ring of bases which the West has thrown around it appears designed rather to contain it as a continent than to be the springboard for operations against the Soviet *bloc*.

This leads us to the second aspect of spatial factors—the control of communication routes. Although there are vast land spaces within the Western world, it is primarily a maritime empire. Sea communications are vital to it because the groups of nations of which it is made up are separated by the oceans, and because most of its supplies of raw materials have to be brought by sea. By contrast, the USSR and its satellites constitute the largest single geo-political unit held by any one group, covering 180 degrees of longitude from the north pole to the seventeenth parallel. The Soviet *bloc* occupies most of the Eurasiatic Island (World Island or Heartland according to the Scotch geo-political writer Makinder). Thus, its interest in sea space is a less vital one; it gets most of its supplies from the continent. But because the seas are of such vital interest to the West they are, indirectly, of strategic interest to possible adversaries of the West who, in case of conflict, would want to be able to disrupt its sea communications.

Now it happens that the underdeveloped countries have considerable strategic importance as regards control of the seas. In the first place, between them they have a large part of the total coastal length of the world. This by itself does not mean very much; what is important is the situation of the coasts in question.

To start with, they have a large share of the coasts, bordering on and capable of blockading Eurasia on the east and the south. The underprivileged nations command the access of the Communist world to the oceans. The only ocean to which the USSR has a long coastline is the Arctic. The Soviets did, indeed, obtain at Yalta the Kurile Islands in return for their last-minute intervention against Japan, and this gave them an outlet into the Pacific. But it was the victory of Communism in China which gave the Communist world a coastline 3,000 kilometres long on to the China seas. Nevertheless, communications between these seas and the Pacific itself are controlled by the many scattered islands which, from Japan to the Philippines, are allied to the West, and even beyond the Philippines are neutral. Very many of the battles for the allegiance of one or other of the underdeveloped Asiatic countries during the last ten years can be interpreted as thrusts of the Russo-Chinese *bloc* towards a sea outlet.

Part of the coastline in which the West has a vital strategic interest for reasons of communication also belongs to underdeveloped countries. In the first place, as long as the West still controls the Pacific islands that ocean is for practical purposes a Western lake and could be used if operations were undertaken against the Communist *bloc*. In the second place, the usual communications route between the major partners in the Western alliance, North

America and Western Europe, is the north Atlantic, but the alternative route passing east of the Antilles, the north coast of Brazil and a line from Pernambuco to Dakar has the advantage of an Atlantic crossing only one third as long as, and much less exposed than, the North Atlantic one. The importance of the various Latin American and Black African states abutting on the two ends of this major communications route is thus evident. Thirdly, Suez and Panama are controlled by underdeveloped countries, even though the Panama Canal itself is a small zone belonging to the United States and, in contrast with the poverty ruling in Panama itself, resembles a little North American island in one of the most destitute corners of Latin America. And Malacca, Singapore and Indonesia control communications routes between the Pacific and Indian oceans.

Lastly, spatial factors have a third aspect bound up with the part played by the sheer territorial extent of such countries. Against modern means of destruction, dispersal offers the best chance of safeguarding strategic and logistic potential. It can be sought either in the oceans or in the vast land masses which are to be found precisely in some of the underdeveloped continents. When these spaces are in addition desert or semi-desert, the necessary equipment can be sited in them without excessive risk to the population either from nuclear industry or by its becoming a target area. Space is also needed for modern weapons tests; nuclear explosions and missile proving call for a great deal of space.[1] And the increased power of destructive weapons, together with the increased range of the means of attack, lead to the setting up of defence in considerable depth so as to reduce the incidence of surprise attack. Russia uses for this purpose the Siberian hinterland but North America, separated from Western Europe by the Atlantic, cannot really act as a proper strategic base. It is Africa, both far enough away from the coasts of Europe and also near

[1] As regards the second point, which is less widely appreciated than the first, the following example may be cited: in order to test guided weapons over distances comparable to that from New York to Moscow, the United States has had to set up a "laboratory" extending from Patrick Base in Florida as far as Ascension Island in the South Atlantic, and this has necessitated delicate negotiations with a number of Latin American countries.

enough to them, which would seem to offer the required theatre for operations in depth.

The underdeveloped countries then, as suppliers of raw materials and of human reserves, and above all of space and communications, are of vital importance for any possible future war. But their political importance is not limited to this potential strategic interest. Even if the advance of military techniques should completely abolish this interest, every one of the great modern countries would want its sphere of influence to cover as much as possible of the underprivileged world even though no tangible benefit, whether military, economic or other, resulted from this. For there is something inherent in the nature of the great human societies that makes them wish to enlarge their spheres of influence, to make their presence felt beyond their borders in a variety of ways and to spread their language, their philosophy of life and their civilization over as large an area as possible. Both the Soviet and the Western camps have superimposed a more or less pronounced ideological pattern on this biological expansion and are the champions, if not of a certain form of political organization, at least of certain principles basic to political organization. In other words, besides the strategic aspects the biological and philosophical aspects of the struggle for the allegiance of the underprivileged nations should not be overlooked.

This desire of the great powers to exercise influence in the underdeveloped countries can be shown arithmetically by the voting in international organizations, which often has the character of a farce. The adherents of each camp can be counted, and the success or otherwise of attempts to seduce them from their allegiance made clear to all. On such occasions a startling light is cast on the relations between the most highly developed countries and the backward ones. "The delegates of underdeveloped states may not yet form a majority in the international organizations, but they are already a large minority which is constantly growing and whose support the great Powers wish to ensure. This contest is particularly clear as between Russia and the United States, but they are by no means the only great Powers who engage in it. Western European powers have no scruples about using the same methods as far as their shrunken means allow. Thus there is set up within organizations which could and should have cherished a spirit of calm and disinterestedness in a disturbed world, a poisoned atmosphere of demagogic competition and sordid bargaining."[1]

[1] Paul Rivet, *Indépendance et Libertie—"Le Monde"* 1st February 1957.

Chapter Fifteen

THE ECONOMIC STAKES

THE INTEREST which the industrialized nations have in the underdeveloped ones both as sellers and as buyers has been touched upon frequently in the preceding chapters. We shall now endeavour to make an overall assessment of it.

Firstly, the underdeveloped countries are a very important source of supply for the industrialized ones. In 1960 44 per cent of United States purchases were made in non-industrialized countries, that is, countries other than North America, Western Europe and Eastern Europe, and Japan. The percentage for France is the same, 44; for Japan it is 51, and for Great Britain 52. When it is borne in mind that the national products of the underdeveloped nations amount together to only between twelve and fifteen per cent of the world total of national products, the significance of these proportions is obvious. It is a measure of the importance of the backward countries as suppliers of raw materials and foodstuffs.

We saw above[1] that vegetable products from underdeveloped countries are not in general of vital importance, at least in the sphere of alimentation. Nor should it be forgotten how quickly substitutes are being developed. Their use has already gone very far in textiles and in rubber, and may soon spread to other pro-

[1] Compare Chapter I, p. 14.

ducts; there is already talk of a synthetic cocoa. By contrast, the importance of the underdeveloped countries, especially the tropical zones, in regard to minerals and hydroelectric resources appears to be on the increase.[1]

Now is the time for the underdeveloped countries to seize the chance which their key position in supplying the world with oil, iron, aluminium and water power offers them to achieve development quickly. *Le temps du monde fini*—which as everybody knows began under Paul Valéry—*va maintenant finir*. This is not only because humanity now looks forward to an interplanetary future. Even on our own world we seem to be nearing the commencement of an age in which the very idea of limitation of resources will vanish. Coal and oil are limited, but solar energy and nuclear fusion energy are not. Moreover, man's progressive mastery over matter is tending to blur the distinctions between different raw materials. In their possession of certain essential raw materials the underdeveloped countries have indeed a trump card, but it is one that should be played quickly.

Underdeveloped countries are also good customers of the industrialized ones. France makes 43 per cent of her purchases in non-industrialized countries as defined on the previous page; the United States make 49 per cent, Britain 51 per cent and Japan 58 per cent.

The importance of the underdeveloped countries resides not only in the immediate outlet they offer for the products of industrialized countries, but even more the potential size of their market. It was not by chance that President Truman's celebrated declaration in 1949, since known as the Point Four Plan, coincided with the first signs of the post-war depression (which, however, was terminated by the Korean crisis a year and a half later). At the same period, a group of experts commissioned by the UNO to study the conditions for full employment in industrialized countries replied by stressing the desirability of world economic expansion, "in which the most important single factor would be the economic development of underdeveloped countries."[2]

[1] Compare Chapter X, pp. 111-116.
[2] UNO doc. E/1584-1949. (No. 1949 II A 3).

Industrialized countries frequently do not sufficiently realize that any aid which they may give to underdeveloped countries, though it may at first look like a sacrifice on their part, is also of vital importance in stimulating their own economies. We shall try to show this by taking the most simple case, that of assistance given to finance investments. The same argument, *mutatis mutandis,* is valid for other forms of aid, particularly for the revaluation of raw materials purchased in underdeveloped countries.

Such assistance inevitably gives rise to orders for industrial products, for the financing of investment contains two separate elements. There is on the one hand the supply of certain goods such as machines, cement, steel products, etc., and on the other hand payment for certain work done locally such as the installation of machinery, civil engineering works, etc. Thus it has been calculated that for French investments made in overseas countries the supply of goods represented 36 per cent of the total and local work 64 per cent (this does not include the mammoth projects). Now it is evident that in an underdeveloped country, whilst the installation and civil engineering work is done locally, a very large part of the capital goods have to be imported from abroad, thus giving rise to the most obvious category of orders.

But if the local work is examined closely it will be seen that this too gives rise to orders from abroad.[1] Let us suppose that the United States finance an investment in Brazil. Disregarding the supply of materials and goods, consider only the financing of local work. The United States can only give dollars, whilst the Brazilian workman has to be paid in cruzeiros. Thus there has to be an exchange medium between the dollars and the cruzeiros. The only convenient method is for the American government to buy goods in the United States with dollars and then sell them or have them sold to Brazil for cruzeiros.[2] This is the well known mechan-

---

[1] The following analysis is also valid for that part of the goods and materials needed for the investment in question which are not imported because they are obtainable locally.

[2] Another procedure could of course be envisaged. American dollars could be set aside by the Brazilian government, which would issue cruzeiros backed by this reserve. But this obviously is a method to be avoided. The existence of a reserve of dollars will not prevent the additional issue of cruzeiros from

ism of *exchange value*; the exchange value in local currency is used for the investment whilst the dollar aid is used for the supply of American goods to Brazil, though not necessarily capital goods. This is a second opportunity, and one not so obvious at first glance, for the country which is giving the aid, to export its products. One of the favourite ideas of the FAO is based on this technique; it is that world agricultural surpluses should be given to underfed countries, which are also underequipped countries, to enable them to finance equipment schemes with the exchange value arising therefrom.

Clearly then aid resolves itself into a gift of goods or, which comes to the same thing, of services.[1]

But the effects of such aid are not limited to export of products to an equivalent amount by the giving country. The additional demand set up in the country giving the aid far exceeds

having an inflationary influence, because a corresponding quantity of goods is not put into circulation. In reality, in such a case, the financing of the Brazilian investment is based on a monetary injection, a thing which in certain cases is not a bad method. As for the American dollars, since they are taken out of their monetary circulation in the United States they have a deflationary effect complementary to the inflationary effect in Brazil.

[1] It would appear at first sight that the analysis which has just been made in the case of the United States and Brazil is not applicable as between two countries belonging to the same monetary area, at least when there is complete, or almost complete, freedom of movement for goods and capital, and stable and unlimited convertibility between the various currencies in the area, which in effect really constitute a single currency. If for example, we look at France and Madagascar, there is no need for the exchange value mechanism to come into play for France to give aid to Madagascar, since the currency is the same. But even in such a case, reflection will show that the aid is equivalent to the gift of goods or services. Assuming that in a given period France gives 10,000 million francs to Madagascar, but that over the same period the disequilibrium in the balance of products and services between them amounts only to 6,000 million in France's favour; then the aid which France has in fact given equals six and not ten thousand million, that being the nett amount contributed from France's national product in favour of Madagascar. The other 4,000 million would represent a deflationary phenomenon in France and an equal inflationary phenomenon in Madagascar, in the same way as in the case examined in note 1 above.

In fact, if as between France and Madagascar it does not seem so essential for French products to be supplied to Madagascar as it would be for American products to be supplied to Brazil in the above illustration, this is because the goods are, as it were, always being supplied; there is a constant flow of French goods to Madagascar because both countries belong to the same monetary area. In other words, in the case of the United States and Brazil, the volume of goods acting as the vehicle for the gift is specific to the operation in question, whereas in the case of France and Madagascar this volume is submerged in a larger and more complex whole.

the amount of the aid itself, because four multipliers come into play.

The first multiplier operates in the giving country because the orders directly due to the aid give rise to others, unless of course they relate to an industrial sector which because of bottlenecks cannot increase its total output. (Neither would this first multiplier come into play if aid were given from surplus stocks, such as excess agricultural products.)

Secondly, investment in the giving country leads to further investment, as was mentioned in Chapter IX[1] and this leads to the possibility of further orders.

The two multipliers just mentioned come into play only once, that is to say in the months immediately after the investment made possible by external aid is put to work. But there are two other multipliers whose effect lasts for years after the investment.

The third multiplier is this : by developing the receiving country, the investment increases its demand for imported products. The incomes distributed in the new factories or new agricultural enterprises are spent in a way which causes some goods to be imported.

These too are only direct incomes distributed by the newly created enterprises themselves. But these primary incomes give rise locally to secondary, tertiary and further incomes, and at every stage part of the incomes is spent on imported products. This then is the fourth multiplier.

The second, third and fourth multipliers just mentioned affect the receiving country. It follows that it is not necessarily the giving country which benefits from these orders. But if the two countries belong to the same monetary area and the same economic grouping, most of these orders will inevitably go to the giving country. If, however, as is generally the case, the two countries do not belong to the same monetary area, the additional orders thus created may benefit third countries. This then des-

[1] One might be tempted to say that this induced investment, which figures under national savings, simply shifts expenditure from one place to another. But in a situation of chronic under-employment, the saving in question is really produced by an effort which is wholly or largely an additional one.

troys the argument, but only from a strictly bilateral point of view. Looking at the industrialized countries as a whole, the effect of economic stimulation will not be lost. This is one more reason why aid to underdeveloped countries should be planned on a concerted basis among the giving or lending nations.

Thus aid can be economically effective not only in those nations which receive it but also in those that give it—though this statement requires two qualifications.

In the first place, if aid were to be given simply because of the stimulating reaction it has in the giving country it might be thought reasonable to give it only spasmodically, in order to counteract weakening tendencies in the industrial countries themselves, whereas of course to be of the greatest benefit to the receiving countries aid must be given without undue interruption. Nevertheless, there would be nothing against mounting an additional aid programme at periods of low economic activity, provided that this did not constitute the total effort but was additional to it.[1]

Secondly, and most importantly, the governments of modern industrialized countries have many other methods at their disposal for stimulating their economies than the indirect one of giving aid to underdeveloped countries. It is Keynes's analysis which shows us the stimulating effect on the giving country. But it was Keynes himself who also taught us that the same technique can be applied within the industrialized nation itself. In other words, *at the same time as he illuminated for us the prophecy of the Marxists*[2] regarding the vital necessity of overseas markets for a capitalist economy, *Keynes delivered us from its inevitability.* The potential market of a depressed economy is primarily within itself. Its economic living space can be found within its own frontiers.

The most one can add to the above remarks is that it is pos-

---

[1] In Chapter II, pp. 21-22 one means of giving such periodic aid was considered—namely, to vary the amount given or lent according to changes in the price of the basic raw materials produced by the underdeveloped countries in question, by reference to standard prices.

[2] Not Marx himself but Rosa Luxembourg and Lenin.

sible, and may one day be scientifically proved, that the stimulating effect is in certain cases more marked, for a given expenditure, if one or several underdeveloped countries are used as intermediaries. It may be that under-employment, which is far more prevalent in new countries, results in a much greater multiplier effect.

However this may be, and subject to what has just been said, the same thing could happen in the relations between nations as has been happening over the last century in the relations between social classes. Why have Marx's prophecies about these relations not been borne out by events? First, because of the Trade Union Movement which ended the weakness of the workman *vis-à-vis* his employer, whereas it had been considered as an essential part of his situation. Then because capitalism has developed in a direction symbolized by Ford, based upon the startling discovery that high wages are in the long run the only way to keep business going.

For a number of years now a kind of Trades Unionism has been growing among the poorer nations—a sort of spirit of Bandung.

But what the industrialized countries have not yet realized is that Fordism can also work in international relations, and that it consists in stabilizing the prices of raw materials at a sufficiently remunerative level and in giving generously towards investment. Industrialized countries cannot fail to recover any outlays they make for this purpose; they already know this, but they still act as though they did not believe it.

Chapter Sixteen

WORLD AID FOR A WORLD PROBLEM

THERE IS a basic difference between the political motives and the economic ones which were examined in the two preceding chapters. The political reasons for the action of industrialized nations relate to a state of conflict, actual or possible, between two coalitions. The two *blocs* are also rivals in the economic sphere, but their rivalry is not fundamental to the action they take. If an underdeveloped country receives assistance towards financing its investments from both sides the two efforts do not cancel one another out, but reinforce one another. Other things being equal development takes place more rapidly, as does trade, and the two groups of industrial countries are simultaneously creating the possibility of commercial expansion for both of them.

In so far as relations between developed countries and under-developed ones are governed by political calculations, they are imprisoned within an idea of aid to underdeveloped countries which is based upon struggle—dominated, that is, by the conflict between the two *blocs*. If on the contrary the political stakes give way to the economic stakes, a struggle between the two *blocs* is no longer of necessity the basic motive. We can rise from the idea of struggle to a *universal conception* of aid.

In this last chapter we shall try to trace the path from the conflict-idea to the universal one.

At present, the policy of industrial nations *vis-à-vis* the underdeveloped ones is dictated by the idea of struggle. Consciously or unconsciously, every action of the rich nations towards the poor ones is in some degree inspired by the struggle between the East and the West, a struggle in which the underdeveloped countries are at once the prize and the judge.

What are the main advantages held by each side in this contest?

One of the trump cards held by the Russians is the clumsiness of the West. Western Europe, or at least the westernmost nations in Western Europe, Great Britain, France and Benelux, find it hard to make that change in their method of dealing with the underdeveloped countries which the progress of ideas has made necessary. Conversely, the United States do not always realize how complex the problems are and often take up rigid anti-colonialist positions too quickly, whilst themselves provoking hostile reactions due to the feeling of economic servitude which they cannot avoid giving to the underdeveloped countries having close relations with them.

But the Communist group has some better cards than these. To begin with, the vast majority of the underprivileged nations are found in Asia, and this gives the USSR the benefit of a feeling of continental solidarity since she herself is an Asiatic power. One quarter of the inhabitants of the USSR, or fifty million people, are in Asia; the USSR has made Siberia and Central Asia one of the great industrial centres of the world, or rather, the theatre of a number of the great industrial centres. Much of Soviet heavy industry is situated close to Iran, Afghanistan, Sinkiang, Mongolia and the Sea of Japan, whilst more than half the steel in the Soviet Union comes from beyond the Urals.

China, as a purely Asiatic nation, is still better placed to spread Communism in Asia; Russians do not form close colonies outside their own borders, whereas the Chinese do. Moreover, the Chinese have the advantage of being coloured. Lastly, it is possible that in China Communism will have a more humane character than in the USSR. Foreign aid coming from the other Communist countries (something which Russia never had) may help to make the road to development less austere. And Chinese humanism traditionally has a happier idea of mankind than has Slav humanism.

But the Communist *bloc's* main advantage is the fact that it offers a "development model" which looks satisfactory. By this is meant a plan which other nations are invited to copy in carrying out their own development. The features of this model are well known : austerity for the individual, agrarian reform, the collective organization of agriculture, state ownership, emphasis on basic industries, and socialist planning. This model exercises a real attraction on underdeveloped countries—so much so that Monsieur Tibor Mende could maintain that Communism's major advantage in the modern world was no longer the hope of a revolutionary change within the industrialized nations, but instead the effort to make non-industrialized countries follow this "model".[1]

Many writers, especially Marxist ones, have considered that it was an accident of history that Communism won its first victories with the Russian revolution instead of starting (for example) with revolution in Germany. By a paradox, the dictatorship of the proletariat was inaugurated by an under-industrialized country. Will the accident of forty years ago become the rule of tomorrow? It is probable, writes Monsieur Tibor Mende[2] "that the more a Communist ideology seems inappropriate to the needs of developed industrial societies, the more it will tend to exploit the role it can still play as a method of economic emancipation in backward agrarian countries."

Let us see on what examples this model of development relies for its good reputation. From Eastern Europe, in spite of some successes, at least in certain spheres such as that of industrialization, it has enjoyed only a limited penetration into underdeveloped countries outside Europe, since by tradition Eastern European countries, squeezed as it were between Western Europe and Russia, do not maintain very close links with such countries. It should

---

[1] *Entre la peur at l'espoir* pp. 27-32 and pp. 121-37.
[2] ibid., pp. 30-31.

also be remembered that as far as penetration is concerned, Eastern Europe bears the stigma of the original sin of conquest and military occupation.

The prestige of the Russian model of development rests primarily upon Russia herself. For although her modern development was already adumbrated in 1917 she claims, not without reason, to owe the tremendous acceleration of her growth to her political system. It may however be asked whether the Russian myth is not destined to lose its penetrating power in underdeveloped countries, for two reasons.

First of all, with the passing of time Russia tends more and more to appear in the eyes of other nations as an "old rich one" —in other words to suffer the fate which has dogged the United States for the last twenty-five years. In 1970 a large part of the men occupying positions of responsibility in the underdeveloped nations (where it is not unusual to reach responsible positions at an early age) will be persons for whom the name of the USSR evokes what it was already when they were young—a formidable power, the rival of the United States for the domination of the world.

On the other hand, one of the strong points of Soviet propaganda is the fact that the United States do exercise a hegemony, so that until very recent years it could be held that in attacking the American hegemony the USSR was attacking all such attitudes. But Soviet successes will inevitably mean that hegemony will increasingly appear divided, so that the ability to criticise will be more evenly divided between the two groups. The suitor who aspires to become a lover does not usually pose conditions; but assuming that the beloved divorces and marries him, then as the husband he might well venture to forbid her to see any other gallants. The United States will be less and less alone in experiencing the woes which are the other side of the coin of supremacy—the financial burdens, the exasperating ingratitude, and what one might call the Arnolphe complex (in Molière's *Ecole des Femmes* Arnolphe coddles Agnes and shuts her up, but still wants to be loved).

But though the myth of Russia may lose some of its power, the myth of China may well take up the torch. We are not well informed about what is really happening in China, but if in a few years' time it became apparent that she is making forced marches away from her underdeveloped state and from the poverty that has dogged her for centuries, this fact would have tremendous repercussions among the underdeveloped countries.

These then are the trump cards of the Eastern *bloc*; what are those of the West?

First of all there is the attachment of certain underdeveloped countries to one of the great traditions of the West, Christianity or individualistic rationalism.

But the greatest is the real wealth of the West. It is much easier for the 400 million richest people in the world to promote, if they can bring themselves to will it, the development of the 600 million people belonging to their group and even the 600 millions belonging to the neutral or neutralist nations as well, than for the 200 million Russians to sustain the 680 million people belonging to their *bloc* and in addition compete with the West in the neutral countries. Yet, however striking the message of the above figures, they give only an imperfect idea of the reality; they have to be supplemented by the following considerations.

The Soviet standard of life is still below not only that of the inhabitants of the United States but also of Western Europe, Australia and New Zealand—so much so that even by the criterion of national income per head alone it could be maintained that the USSR is not yet a developed country[1] however paradoxical this statement may seem in view of Russia's prodigious success in certain technical and industrial fields. This means that, other things being equal, it is a bigger burden upon a Russian to provide a given amount of aid abroad than on an American or even a Frenchman.

---

[1] If for example the threshold above which a country is termed developed is fixed at 600 or 700 dollars annually per head. Between this limit and that of 200 dollars which was the ceiling proposed for the underdeveloped nations (compare introduction page xviii) we have the "middle class" nations; the USSR, Japan, Argentina, the Union of South Africa.

On the other hand, there are differences between the under-developed countries themselves. Very broadly, Latin America is at present richer than Africa and Africa richer than Asia. Now most of the underdeveloped countries of the Communist world, and among the neutral nations, are in Asia, whilst the under-developed countries having links with the West are about one third South American, one third African and only a third Asiatic.

It is imperative for the countries of the West to realize that they are in possession of the means to ensure successful experi-ments in accelerated development in the non-Communist coun-tries and that, in the context of the idea of competition in re-lations with the under-privileged countries, a resounding success in one or two large underdeveloped regions of the world could by itself in a few years counter-balance in the minds of backward nations the repercussions of China's success, should this come to pass.

It is therefore hard to predict the outcome of the competition between East and West in this vast field. But there is no doubt that so long as rivalry continues between East and West this is bound to be of great consequence to the underdeveloped nations themselves.

In a sense, the cold war enables the underdeveloped countries to rely upon attention to their wants from both sides such as they would hardly be likely to receive without it. It may be that each of the two *blocs* is encouraging growth in underdeveloped coun-tries simply because the other *bloc* exists. This is particularly true just at the present time; but in the longer term, aid given to underdeveloped countries on a competitive basis is exceedingly harmful to them, and this for four reasons.

In the first place, the competitive struggle whittles down world savings and greatly reduces the sums which can be devoted to financing growth in the underdeveloped countries, particularly when we remember that most of our contemporaries still look upon this as an optional expense. The alternative of guns or butter reappears here on a world scale. For the cold war not only diverts the money of industrial countries from aid to underdeveloped ones; it also diverts the funds of the underdeveloped countries themselves from financing their own development; for the poorer countries too are led to indulge in military expenses either because, being members of one camp, they are encouraged to participate in the effort of that camp, or even because of local tensions not owing their origin to the great struggle between East and West but beyond the skill of the great Powers to settle, or even actively fomented by them. All in all, it is a scandalous thought that every year the budgets of the nations of the world contribute 100,000 million dollars to prepare for war and less than six thousand million for aid to underdeveloped countries.

Secondly, the cold war not only reduces aid; it causes it to be distributed according to absurd criteria. It is doubtless right that the United States should devote the majority of its effort to Asia, overpopulated and threatened by famine. But the distribution within Asia should follow a logical pattern. In 1957, out of assistance totalling 1,355 million dollars to underdeveloped countries as a whole, 670 millions or about half, were divided between Formosa (93 million dollars), South Korea (355 million dollars) and South Viet Nam (222 million dollars). These three countries, which together have 40 million inhabitants, received for themselves from the United States as much as all the other inhabitants of non-Communist underdeveloped countries, who number 1,150 millions. The cold war, in fact, causes the two *blocs* to make their greatest effort not where the need is greatest but on the outskirts of the groups for which they consider themselves responsible, as if it had been said: "thou shalt first love the most distant foreigner as thyself."[1]

Thirdly, not only is the aid insufficient and badly distributed, it is also tainted by the spirit of competition. Often the real object is not so much to enable a given underdeveloped country to overcome its problems as to induce it to enter an alliance or virtually to do so, or conversely to dissuade it from entering into a similar arrangement with the other side. This means that

[1] See Chapter IX, p. 98 for the division among the underdeveloped countries of aid coming from all the developed ones.

aid is intermixed with political conditions which up till now the USSR unlike the United States, has been clever enough to disguise. But in 1958 the USSR and Eastern Germany retracted for five years credits which had been promised to Yugoslavia in 1956, simply because the latter was unwilling to join the Eastern camp. Churches of course have always made a distinction between heretics and infidels, usually assigning to the latter a more comfortable place as regards both temporal and eternal punishments. But in spite of this precedent the case of Yugoslavia is bound to make neutral states, whether Asiatic or African, which counted on receiving Soviet aid to overcome their underdevelopment because they were assured that it was free of strings, think twice about it.

Nor is this all; when countries loosen their purse-strings they are so afraid of seeing their protégés escape them that they are not content with a watching brief on their attitude in external affairs. They are also anxious to avoid internal upheavals which may result in alterations to their foreign policies. Although the Americans are convinced on the whole of the usefulness of agrarian reform in most of the underdeveloped countries, they still act particularly in Asia, as if they were thinking : "If I unseat these feudalist, landed proprietors, these swindling merchants, these proliferating rulers, am I not in danger of burying myself beneath the ruins of the temple, like Samson ?"

Fourthly and lastly, the type of relationship which the industrialized countries are setting up with the young and poor nations because of this context of conflict threatens to warp their mentality. Without reviving old-fashioned paternalist ideas, one is entitled to say that the most developed countries have a moral responsibility towards the underdeveloped ones, which are passing through a kind of adolescence not only in the economic sphere but also, at least in many cases, mentally as well. And all too often the way in which aid is given might well lead them secretly to despise the donor, whether justifiably or not. For they see that aid is not necessarily given to the country which can show that it is making personal efforts to further its own growth, or that the aid received will form part of a sound plan of development. They see that other and less logical arguments are more compelling. The arts of innuendo can be employed to hint that one is tempted to yield to advances from another quarter and this does not foster an atmosphere of integrity.

The young and poor nations are in danger of entering upon the stage of history with the mental paraphernalia of prostitutes, and the Big Powers are to blame for this.

These, then, are the reasons why everything possible should be done to prevent relationships with underdeveloped countries from being fatally coloured by the cold war.

When American influence appears strongly in an underdeveloped part of the world, this leads the Soviets to put in an appearance as well, and conversely, so that the rivalry between the two powers soon highlights the competitive nature of the aid. This lends special significance to the part that can be played by other industrialized nations whose presence does not have this effect, at least to the same degree. It is interesting to note that some of the world's underdeveloped areas have come to rely not on one of the two great power *blocs*, but on other industrial powers, especially the nations of Europe. Perhaps it is already too late to consider applying this principle in the Middle East, but it is certainly not too late in Africa, if Europe has courage enough to devote sufficient effort to the development of Africa.

There is another way to avoid the attitude of conflict. This is for all the industrial nations, including the United States and the USSR, to come together on a joint worldwide programme of aid. The problem of developing the poorer nations is so vast that the pooling of all available goodwill and effort would barely suffice to master within the next few decades this problem, aggravated as it will be by the end of the century through the worldwide demographic explosion into a veritable nightmare. The great contribution of the United States would be its resources and its intellectual honesty. The USSR, China and some Western European countries such as Great Britain, France, Belgium and Holland could bring their experience in the art of development.

Instead of seeking out ways of nullifying each other's efforts, today's protagonists would all come together to collaborate in one or several world organizations. It would be child's play to draw up a plan for such organizations; that is not where the difficulty lies. Nothing will be easier than to work out the necessary structure and procedure, once the nations have really made up their minds to carry out the task together.

The work of these organizations would have to be based on a few simple principles which we have attempted to set out in the preceding chapters. The main points may be recalled here. The first task for the developed countries, both logically and in order of time, is to stabilize the prices of raw materials, in agreement with the underdeveloped countries, at a sufficiently remunerative level for the producer. This could be done by setting up both agreements for each product or group of products and techniques whereby deficits incurred by the national revenues of the underdeveloped countries during periods of low economic activity (or in respect of all the main products involved) would be financially bridged.

The naïve idea of private investment as a panacea should be given up, since on the contrary it is inadequate to deal with the majority of the most urgent and important tasks. Nevertheless, wherever it is acceptable it can render considerable service, especially in countries whose growth has already reached a certain minimum level; but an international system of guarantees is required to ensure its rapid expansion.

Underdeveloped countries should not start with the assumption that it is an evil thing for industrialized countries to exploit their raw materials. The local government should rather judge such activity in terms of its economic profitability.

The ways and means of growth, which would be both economic and social and nearly always agricultural and industrial too, have to be determined for each nation as a special case. With the support of the intellectual aid received, each nation should draw up its own plan and finance it initially by its own efforts. Aid from outside should be integrated into this plan and fused with the effort. All that outside donors or leaders are entitled to ask is that the plan exists, the effort is afoot, and that the proposed projects will stand up to proper examination.

There is an urgent need for a world organization which would finance actual development, to stand between the International Bank which finances financially profitable projects and the many organizations offering intellectual aid. This organization could begin in a small way, and the very difficulty of getting it started[1] should caution us against expecting too much from it at first. But if it is to act on a scale equal to the need, then sooner or later it will have to be founded from an international tax based on each nation's *per capita* income.

Lastly, the financing of development does not mean only supplying the material equipment needed for growth; it also means financing agrarian reform, the establishment of co-opera-tives and (in many cases at least) the teaching and the supplies needed for birth control.

To advocate concerted worldwide action is not to despise regional action based on special relationships between two or more countries having geographical or historical ties. For whilst the worldwide structure is still a-building, such activity is good and indispensable, and will always have a more human aspect than that of the global organizations. Even if international justice with universal taxation becomes the order of the day, there will remain many a problem which is best solved within the framework of a smaller grouping.[2]

But however much such supplementary activities may contri-bute, however fruitful the relationships between industrialized countries and backward ones (and they must of course be new-

---

[1] The International Development Association has some claims to be con-sidered as a respectable embryo of such an organization, even though the USSR is not a member.

[2] For instance, in the compartmentalized world in which the rich countries seal off their frontiers, the only large population movements still possible are within certain communities, where incidentally they sometimes raise serious problems. Such are the movement of people from the British West Indies to the suburbs of London, of Algerians into the larger towns in France, and of Puerto Ricans who form an increasing proportion of the New York slum dwellers.

model relationships), a real world organization will still be needed. For only the creation of such an organization will prove that the rich nations of the world have given up an exclusive concern with themselves, with pride and avarice as their only companions.

La Bruyère remarked how we feel almost ashamed at enjoying good fortune within sight of certain kinds of unhappiness.[1] The main excuse of the rich nations is their lack of imagination; confronted with the extreme of human misery, they remain unaware of it. The blaze of the chandeliers conceals from the fortunate guests the faces of the poor in the night outside. Or rather, we live on Olympus (the ancients, in their attempt to describe the origin of humanity, were unwittingly prophesying the future). Olympus exists, and we are on it. The gods and demi-gods have all the vices of humanity, but they eat and drink of the best and have all that heart could wish for. Ordinary human beings (that is to say, the vast majority of the earth's inhabitants) are dependent for much of their chance of happiness upon the goodwill of these gods and demi-gods; but the latter are almost wholly taken up with their own quarrels and, as in the Iliad, draw mankind into their respective camps.

But perhaps the Olympians will one day come to see that the achievement of happiness for mankind is a sufficiently exalted task to justify even the gods in composing their differences.

[1] Chapter XI, "De L'homme". No. 82.

BIBLIOGRAPHY

1. BOOKS

Samir AMIN. *Les effets structurels de l'intégration internationale des économies précapitalistes* (a theoretical study of the process whereby so-called undeveloped economics come into being). Aix-en-Provence, Office universitaire de Polycopie, 1957.

Georges BALANDIERG. *Sociologie Actuelle de l'Afrique Noire*. The dynamics of social change in Central Africa, Paris, P.U.F. 1955.

ID. *L'Anthropologie appliquée aux problémes des pays sous-développés*. Paris, Cours de Droit, 1955.

Georges BALANDIER and others. *Le "tiers monde"*. Underdevelopment and development. Paris, P.U.F. 1956.

Chester BOWLES. *The New Dimensions of Peace*. New York, Harper, 1956.

Norman S. BUCHANAN and Howard S. ELLIS. *Approaches to Economic Development*, New York. The Twentieth Century Fund, 1955.

Josué DE CASTRO. *Géopolitique de la Faim*, Paris, Les Editions ouvrières, Economie et humanisme, 1952.

Aimé CÉSAIRE. *Discours sur le colonialisme*, 2nd edition, Paris, Présence africaine, 1955.

Colin CLARKE. *The Conditions of Economic Progress*, London, Macmillan, 1940 (3rd edition 1957).

René DUMONT. *Economie agricole dans le monde*, Paris, Dalliz, 1954.

ID. *Révolution dans les campagnes chinoises*, Paris, Les Edition du Seuil 1957.

Jean EHRHARD. *Le destin du colonialisme*, Paris, Editions Eyrolles, 1957.

S. Herbert FRANKEL. *The Economic Impact on Underdeveloped Societies.* Essays on international investment and social change. Oxford, Basil Blackwell, 1953.

ID. *Some Conceptual Aspects of International Economic Development of Underdeveloped Territories,* Princeton, University Press, 1952.

Maurice LENGELLÉ and Michel CÉPÈDE. *L'Economie de l'alimentation,* Paris, P.U.F. 1955.

William Arthur LEWIS. *The Theory of Economic Growth,* London. George Allen & Unwin, 1955.

ID. *Report on Industrialization and the Gold Coast,* Accra Gold Coast Government, 1953.

G. MARCY. *Variations du change et termes de l'échange dans la théorie économique contemporaine* (report presented at the Colleque de Royaument in 1955, roneoed).

Albert MEMMI. *Portrait du colonisé,* preceded by *Portrait du colonisateur,* Paris, Buchet-Chastel, Correa, 1957.

Tibor MENDE. *L'Inde devant l'orage,* Paris Editions du Seuil, 1950.

ID. *La révolte de l'Asie,* Paris, P.U.F. 1952.

ID. *L'Amérique Latine entre en scène,* Paris, Editions du Seuil, 1952.

ID. *L'Asie du Sud-Est entre deux mondes,* Paris, Editions du Seuil, 1954.

ID. *Regards sur l'histoire de demain,* Paris, Editions du Seuil, 1954.

ID. *Conversations avec Nehru,* Paris, Editions du Seuil, 1956.

ID. *Entre la peur et l'espoir, réflexions sur l'histoire d'aujourd'hui,* Paris, Editions du Seuil, 1958.

Pierre MOUSSA. *Les chances économiques de la Communauté franco-africaine,* Paris, Armand Colin, 1957.

Gunnar MYRDAL. *Une économie internationale,* Paris, P.U.F. 1958.

ID. *Development and Underdevelopment* (A note on the mechanism of national and international economic inequality). Cairo, National Bank of Egypt, 1956.

Ragnar NURKSE. *Problems of capital formation in an underdeveloped.* Oxford, Basil Blackwell, 1953.

K. L. PANIKKAR. *L'Asie et la domination occidentale du XVe siècle à nos jours,* Paris, Editions du Seuil, 1953.

W. W. ROSTOW. *The Process of Economic Growth.* Oxford. Clarendon Press, 1953.

Alfred SAUVY. *Théorie, générale de la population,* Paris, P.U.F. Vol. 1 : *Economie et population.* 1952.
Vol. II : *Biologie sociale,* 1954.

Germaine TILLION. *L'Algérie en 1957,* Paris, Editions de Minuit 1957.

Jan TINBERGEN. *The Design of Development*. The Economic Development Institute, International Bank of Reconstruction and Development, Baltimore, The Johns Hopkins Press, 1958.

William VOGT, *La faim du monde* (Road to survival), Paris, Hachette, 1950.

Richard WRIGHT. *Bandoeng, 1500 000 000 d'hommes*, Paris, Calmann-Lévy, 1955.

2. REVIEWS AND PERIODICALS

American economic review:
May 1952 : Ragnar NURKSE. Some international aspects of the problems of economic development.

Legal, political, economic and social records. (Faculty of Law, Algiers). 1957, No. 2 : Pierre FONTANEU. Essays on investment.

Bulletin of the scholars' and old scholars' association of rue Saint-Guillaume.
1957 : René DUMONT. La réforme agraire et la coopération agricole en Chine.

International Bulletin of the Social Sciences (UNESCO) :
Vol. III No. 1. Spring 1951 : Colin CLARKE—Terms of exchange in the future.
Vol VI No. 2. 1954 : Simon KUZNETS—Population, income and capital.

S.E.D.E.I.S. Bulletin.
1.12.1955 : Bertrand DE JOUVENEL. La contribution de l'agriculture à l'essor de la production industrielle et du niveau de vie.
15.3.1958 : Paul HUMBLOT. Evolution demographique et problèmes de l'economie les pays de la zone franc.

Cahiers de la République:
1956. No. 2; Pierre MENDÈS-FRANCE. Le problèmes des pays sous-développés et la politique internationale.
1956. No. 3 : Gunnar MYRDAL. Développement et sous-développement.
Ibid : Tibor MENDE. Réflexions sur une attitude nouvelle devant le defi lancé par les régions sous-développées.
May-June 1957 : Robert BURON. Les problèmes du sous-développement et l'assistance technique.

Civilizations:
   1956. No. 1 : G. Ugo PAPI. Théorie du développement économique et de la formation des zones arriérées.

Economie appliquée:
   April-September 1947 : Simon KUZNETS. Les différences internationales dans la formation du capital et son financement.
   June 1954 : Paul ROSENSTEIN-RODAN. Les besoins de capitaux dans les pays sous-développés.

Esprit:
   May 1956 : Alain BERGER. Un milliard d'hommes qui ne veulent pas attendre.
   January 1957 : Tibor MENDE. L'Occident face aux pays de l'Islam.
   June 1957. Special number on "les maladier infantiles de l'indépendence" (teething troubles of independence).

Etudes et conjoncture: (Institute national de la Statistique et des Etudes économiques) :
   Special extra issue 1951 : Quelques aspects fondamentaux de l'économie mondiale.
   November 1956. Robert BURON. Le développement des pays sous-développés. L'avenir de l'Afrique Noire.

Hommes et Commerce:
   June-July 1955 : Maurice-François ROUGÉ. L'âge de la géonomie.

Indian Economic Review:
   February 1952 : V.K.R.V. RAO. Investment, income and the multiplier in an underdeveloped economy.
   August 1952 : V.K.R.V. RAO. Full employment and economic development.
   Ibid. H. W. SINGER. The mechanics of economic development. A quantitative model approach.

Interamerican Economic Affairs:
   Summer 1956 : P. T. ELLSWORTH. The terms of trade between primary producing and industrial countries.

Nouvelles de l'Europe. (International bulletin of the European Movement.
   August-Sept. 1956 : André PHILIP. *L'Europe et les pays sous-développés* (report to the last European Labour Congress.)

Politique étrangerè:
   1957. No. 3; Charles BETTELHEIM. Sous-développement et planification.
   Ibid : Georges BALANDIER. Les conditions sociologiques du développement.
   1957. No. 5 : Rene SERVOISE. Problèmes internationaux du sous-développement.

Population:
October 1951 : Alfred SAUVY. Introduction a l'étude des pays sous-développés.

October-December 1953 : Alfred SAUVY. Les populations du monde et les besoins en matières premières.

April 1955 : Jean SUTTER. Le mouvement dans le monde en faveur de la limitation des familles.

Review of Economic Progress:
April-June 1952 : Colin CLARKE. The economy of underdeveloped countries.

Revue de la défense nationale:
February 1956 : Général DE LA CHAPELLE. Les aspects particuliers de la guerre possible.

Ibid : General MARCHAND. Stratégie et psychologie en Afrique Noire.

May 1957 : Amiraglio di Squadra G. FIORAVANZO. La mer dans la stratégie des grands espaces.

Ibid : Rene GRANDCHAMP. Défense ultra-moderne des deux Ameriques.

April 1957 : Ingénieur général COMBAUX. Au delà de Clausewitz.

Ibid : Colonel Louis DULLIN. Est-ce la fin d'un système de défense?

July 1957 : General Ch. AILLERET. Illusion ou réalité de l'arme absolue.

December 1957 : Ingénieur général COMBAUX. Necessité d'une Eurafrique.

Ibid : Ingénieur principal CORBEAU. Aperçus techniques et militaires sur les "spoutniki".

February 1958 : Contre-amiral LEPOTIER. Géopolitique et géostratégie.

March 1958 : General Ch. AILLERET. Guerre nucléaire limitée ou "drôle de guerre".

Ibid : Colonel PARISOT. Valeur stratégique de l'Afrique pour l' OTAN.

Revue d'économie politique:
May-June 1955 : Alain BARRÈRE. L'analyse des relations entre le capital et la production.
(Report to Congress of French-speaking Economists).

May-June 1957 : Maurice BYÉ. L'autofinancement de la grande unité interterritoriale et les dimensions temporelles de son plan (Report to Congress of French-speaking Economists).

Revue International du Travail: (International Labour Review) :
May 1958 : Problèmes d'investissement dans les pays insuffisamment développés. (Also available in English).

August 1958 : Méthodes de production et création d's emplois dans les économies insuffisamment développés.

Revue de science financière:
January-March 1957 : BLOCH. L'Assistance technique des Nations Unies en matière financière.

3. PUBLICATIONS OF THE ISEA
(Institute of Applied Economic Science)

1955. D. No. 8 : François PERROUX. *Matériaux pour une analyse de la croissance économique.*

F. Nos. 1 and 2. G. DESTANNE DE BERNIS, François PERROUX, J. DE LARGENTAYE and Maurice BYÉ, K. MARTIN and L. RIST. *Niveaux de développement et politique de croissance.* Introduction à leur étude.

1956 and 1957. F. No. 3 : J. H. FURTH, J. H. ADLER, C. P. KINDLEBERGER, E. VARGA and J. MOULY. *Niveaux de développement et politiques de croissance.*

I. No. 1 : FRANÇOIS PERROUX. *La théorie du progrès économique:* I. *Les mesures des progrès économiques et l'idée d'économie progressive* (1956); II. *Les composants* : 1. La création (1957) : 2. La propagation : A Modèles microéconomiques (1957).

4. LECTURES AND PAPERS

Tibor MENDE. *Les territoires sous-développés; un défi pour l'Occident.* Lecture given at the Inter-allied Union during the Annual Meeting of the General Syndicate of the Jute Industry (November 1954).

Bertrand DE JOUVENEL. *Le développement des pays économiquement arriérés et les problèmes posés à la France.* Address given to the Study and Liaison Committee of the French Union employers organisation (January 1957).

Luc DURAND-REVILLE. *La stabilisation à l'échelon international, des prix des produits de base dans les pays insufissamment développés,* report presented to the Interparliamentary Union (1957).

ID. *Principes devant régir l'investissement, dans les pays en voie de développement économique, de capitaux étrangers provenant de source privée ou gouvernementale, d'une nation déterminée ou d'une organisation internationale,* report presented to the Interparliamentary Union (1958).

Jacques GABORY. *Des pays sous-développés,* January 1958, (roneoed study).

Eugène DEMONT and Paul HUMBLOT. *Évolution démographique et problèmes de l'économie dans la zone franc.* Address to the Study and Liaison Committee of the French Union employers organisation (1958).

5. DOCUMENTS OF THE UNITED NATIONS ORGANIZATION

International capital movements during the interwar period. Doc. ST/ECA/2, 1949 (No. 1949 II.D.2).

Methods whereby the economic development of insufficiently developed countries can be financed. Doc. E/1333, 1949 (No. 1949 II.B 4).

Mesures d'ordre national et international en vue du plein emploi report of a group of experts appointed by the Secretary-General, Doc. E/1584 (No. 1949, II.A.3).

Relative prices of exports and imports of underdeveloped countries, a study of post-war terms of trade between underdeveloped and industrialized countries (No. 1949, II.B.3).

Développement économique des pays insuffisamment développés: méthodes permettant de financer le développement économique des pays insuffisamment développés. A study of the policies influencing investment of foreign private capital. Doc. E/1614, 1950 (unobtainable).

Domestic financing of economic development. Methods of increasing domestic savings and of ensuring their most advantageous use for the purpose of economic development. Doc. ST/ECA/7, 1950 (No. 1951, II.B.1).

Mesures à prendre pour le développement économique des pays insuffisamment développés. Report of a group of experts appointed by the Secretary-General. Doc. E/1986, ST/ECA/10, 1951 (No. 1951, II.B.2).

Développement économique des pays insuffisamment développes: méthodes destinés à accroître la productivité dans le monde. Working paper drawn up by the Secretary-General. Doc. E/2265, 1952 (unobtainable).

Instabilité des marchés d'exportation des pays insuffisamment développés. Rapport entre cette instabilité et la possibilité qu'ont ces pays de se procurer des devises en exportant des produits primaires, 1901 to 1950, Doc. E/2047. ST/ECA/15. 1952 (No. 1952 II.A.1).

Développement économique des pays insuffisamment développés: développement économique intégré. Doc E/2381, 1953 (unobtainable).

Rapport sur un fonds spécial des Nations Unies pour le développement économique. Doc. E/2381. 1953 (No. 1953, II.B.1).

Commerce des produits de base et développement économique. Report of a committee nominated by the Secretary-General. Doc. E/2519, 1953 (No. 1954, II.B.1).

Processus et problèmes de l'industrialisation des pays sous-développés, Doc. E/2670, ST/ECA/29, 1954 (unobtainable).

*Progrès de la réforme agraire. Analyse des reponses des gouvernements à un questionnaire de l'*ONU, Doc. E/2526, ST/ECA/21, 1954 (No. 1954, II.B.3) : Doc. E/2930, ST/ECA/42,1956 No. 1956 II.B.3).

Per Capita National Product of fifty-five countries: 1952-1954, Doc. ST/STAT/SER.E/4, 1956 (No. 1957, XVII. 2).

6. DOCUMENTS OF UNITED NATIONS DEPENDENT ORGANIZATIONS

Rapport sur les investissements internationaux et les possibilités de financement, Food and Agriculture Organization of the United Nations. Doc. C.49/16, 1949 (unobtainable).

Theoretical and practical problems of economic growth, Economic Commission for Latin America, Doc. E/CN.12/221, 1951 (unobtainable).

La situation mondiale de l'alimentation et de l'agriculture, 1956, FAO. Rome, 1956.

Le commerce international en 1956. The contracting parties to the General Agreement on Tariffs and Trade, Geneva, June 1957. (No. G.A.T.T. 1957, 2).

L'homme et la faim, Food and Agriculture Organization of the United Nations, Collection "L'alimentation mondiale," Notebook No. 2 Rome, 1957.

La situation mondiale de l'alimentation et de l'agriculture 1958, Food and Agriculture Organization of the United Nations, Rome, 1958.

La situation mondiale de l'alimantation et de l'agriculture 1961. FAO, Rome, 1961.